The Chronological Word Truth Life
BIBLE

BEHOLD THE LAMB
A Harmony of the Gospels
Second Edition

C. Austin Tucker

ROUTE 66 MINISTRIES

Printed in the United States of America
First Printing: 2016
ISBN 978-0-9890381-2-6

www.Route66Ministries.com

Table of Contents

Introduction to The Chronological Word Truth Life Bible xvii

KJV, NIV, ESV – A Word About Bible Translations xix

Behold The Lamb: An Introduction to This Book xxiii

PART I – JESUS' EARLY YEARS xxiv

Prologue – God Becomes Man 1
    Introduction 1
    The Word Becomes Flesh 1
    Jesus' Genealogy Through Joseph 2
    Jesus' Genealogy Through Mary 3

CHAPTER 1 – The Birth of Christ and Early Years 7
    The Angel Gabriel Predicts John the Baptist's Birth. 7
    Gabriel Predicts Jesus' Birth. 8
    Mary Visits Elizabeth 8
    Mary Praises in Song 9
    John the Baptist Is Born 9
    Zechariah Praises in Song 9
    An Angel Appears to Joseph 10
    Jesus Christ Is Born 10
    An Angel Announces Jesus' Birth to Shepherds. 11
    Jesus' Parents Present Him at the Temple 11
    Wise Men Visit Jesus. 12
    Jesus' Family Escapes to Egypt 12
    Jesus' Family Returns to Nazareth 13
    Young Jesus Stays Behind in Jerusalem. 13

CHAPTER 2 – The Beginning of Jesus' Ministry. 15
    John the Baptist Prepares the Way 15
    John Baptizes Jesus 16
    Satan Tempts Jesus in the Desert 16
    John Denies Being the Christ 17
    John Declares Jesus the Lamb of God 18
    John's Disciples Follow Jesus 18
    Philip and Nathanael Follow Jesus 18
    Jesus Turns Water Into Wine 19
    Jesus Clears the Temple 19
    Jesus Teaches Nicodemus 20
    John Testifies About Jesus 21
    Herod Imprisons John 22

Jesus Talks With a Samaritan Woman 22
The Fields Are Ripe for Harvest 23
Samaritans Believe in Jesus 23

PART II – JESUS' GALILEAN MINISTRY 24

CHAPTER 3 – Teachings and Healings in Galilee & Jerusalem 25
Jesus Begins Teaching in Galilee 25
Jesus Heals the Official's Son 25
The People Reject Jesus at Nazareth 26
Jesus Calls Four Fishermen. 26
Jesus Drives Out a Demon 27
Jesus Heals Peter's Mother-in-Law and Others 28
Jesus Prays in a Secluded Place 28
Jesus Preaches and Heals in Galilee. 28
Jesus Heals a Man's Leprosy 28
Jesus Heals a Paralytic. 29
Jesus Calls Matthew 30
John's Disciples Question Jesus About Fasting. 30
Jesus Heals a Man at Bethesda Pool. 30
Jesus Teaches About His Authority 31

CHAPTER 4 – The Apostles' Call and the Sermon on the Mount. 33
Jesus Demonstrates Lordship Over the Sabbath 33
Jesus Teaches by the Sea. 34
Jesus Chooses 12 Apostles 34
The Sermon on the Mount 35
    The Beatitudes. 35
    Be the Salt of the Earth 35
    Be Light to the World 36
    Jesus Fulfills the Law. 36
    Don't Commit Murder. 36
    Don't Commit Adultery. 37
    Honor Your Promises 37
    Love Your Enemies 37
    Don't Give or Fast for Show. 38
    Store Your Treasures in Heaven 38
    Don't Worry 38
    Judge Without Hypocrisy 39
    Judge a Tree by Its Fruit. 39
    Enter the Narrow Gate 40
    The Wise and Foolish Builders. 40

CHAPTER 5 – Opposition and Parables 41
The Centurion Demonstrates Faith 41
Jesus Raises a Widow's Son 41
John the Baptist Questions Jesus 42
Jesus Condemns Unrepentant Cities 43
A Sinful Woman Anoints Jesus 43
Women Follow Jesus 44
Jesus Heals the Blind and Mute 44
Jesus Is Accused of Alliance With Beelzebub 45
The Jewish Leaders Demand a Sign 46
Jesus' Mother and Brothers Worry About Him 46
The Parable of the Sower 47
The Parable of the Growing Seed 48
The Parables of the Mustard Seed and the Yeast 48
The Parables of the Hidden Treasure and the Pearl 48
The Parable of the Net 48
The Parable of the Wheat and the Weeds 49
Jesus Explains Why He Speaks in Parables 49
Jesus Explains the Parable of the Weeds 50

CHAPTER 6 – Miracles of Nourishment and Nature 51
Jesus Calms the Storm 51
Jesus Heals Two Demon-Possessed Men 51
Jesus Raises a Dead Girl and Heals a Sick Woman 52
Jesus Sends Out the Twelve 53
Herod Has John the Baptist Beheaded 55
Jesus Feeds the 5000 56
Jesus Walks on Water 57
Jesus Is the Bread of Life 58
Many Disciples Desert Jesus 59
Herod Tries to See Jesus 60
Jesus Teaches About What Makes One Unclean 60
A Gentile Woman Has Faith 61
Jesus Heals a Deaf Mute 62
Jesus Feeds the 4000 62
The Jewish Leaders Demand a Sign 62
Jesus Warns Against the Teaching of the Pharisees 63
Jesus Heals a Blind Man at Bethsaida 63
Peter Acknowledges Jesus as the Christ 63
Jesus Predicts His Death and Resurrection 64

CHAPTER 7 – The Transfiguration and Teachings 65
Jesus Is Transfigured 65
Jesus Teaches About Elijah 65
Jesus Heals a Boy of an Evil Spirit 66
Jesus Teaches About Prayer 67
The Parable of the Persistent Widow 68
Jesus Predicts His Death a Second Time 68
Jesus Pays the Annual Temple Tax 68
Jesus' Brothers Question Him 69
Samaritans Oppose Jesus 69
The Cost of Following Jesus 69

PART III – JESUS' LATER JUDEAN MINISTRY 70

CHAPTER 8 – Jesus' Teachings at the Feasts 71
Jesus Attends the Feast of Tabernacles 71
People Wonder If Jesus Is the Christ 72
Jesus Validates His Testimony 73
Jesus Is Greater Than Abraham 73
The Jewish Leaders Refuse to Believe 75
Jesus Forgives an Adulterous Woman 75
Jesus Heals a Man Born Blind 76
Jesus Is the Good Shepherd 77
Jesus Sends Out the 72 78
The Parable of the Good Samaritan 78
Jesus Visits Martha and Mary 79
Jesus Eats Dinner With a Pharisee 79
The Parable of the Rich Fool 80
Jesus Warns People to Repent or Perish 80
Jesus Heals a Crippled Woman on the Sabbath 81
Jewish Opposition at the Feast of Dedication 81

PART IV – JESUS' LATER PEREAN MINISTRY 83

CHAPTER 9 – The Perean Parables 85
Jesus Returns to Perea 85
The Pharisees Warn Jesus 85
Jesus Heals a Man on the Sabbath 85
A Parable of Humility 86
The Parable of the Great Banquet 86
The Cost of Discipleship 87
The Parable of the Lost Sheep 87
The Parable of the Lost Coin 88
The Parable of the Lost Son 88

The Parable of the Clever Manager 89
The Coming of the Kingdom of God 90
The Parable of the Rich Man and Lazarus 90
The Parable of the Unforgiving Servant 91
Jesus Teaches About Forgiveness 92
Being a Servant 92

CHAPTER 10 – Teachings and the Raising of Lazarus 93
Jesus Raises Lazarus From the Dead 93
The Jews Plot to Kill Jesus 95
Jesus Heals Ten Lepers 95
Jesus Teaches About Divorce 95
Jesus Blesses the Children 96
Jesus Teaches the Rich Young Man 97
The Parable of the Vineyard Workers 98
Jesus Predicts His Death and Resurrection a Third Time 98
James and John Make a Request 99
The Disciples Argue About Who's the Greatest 99
Jesus Restores Blind Bartimaeus' Sight 100
Zacchaeus the Tax Collector Repents 100
The Parable of the Ten Minas 101
The Jews Travel to Jerusalem for Passover 102

PART V – JESUS' FINAL WEEK 103

Chapter 11 – Saturday, Sunday, & Monday 105
Mary Anoints Jesus at Bethany 105
The Crowd Welcomes Jesus to Jerusalem 106
Jesus Curses a Fig Tree and Clears the Temple 107
Jesus Predicts His Crucifixion 108

Chapter 12 – Tuesday 111
The Lesson of the Withered Fig Tree 111
The Jewish Leaders Challenge Jesus' Authority 111
The Parable of the Two Sons 112
The Parable of the Greedy Vineyard Farmers 112
The Parable of the Wedding Banquet 113
Jesus Rebukes the Scribes and Pharisees 114
The Jewish Leaders Ask About Paying Taxes to Caesar 115
The Sadducees Ask About Resurrection and Marriage 116
A Pharisee Asks About the Greatest Commandment 116
Whose Son Is the Christ? 117
The Parable of the Pharisee and the Tax Collector 117
A Widow Gives a Sacrificial Offering 117

Signs of the End of the Age 118
Jesus Came to Cause Division 120
The Sheep and the Goats 120
The Parable of the Wise and Foolish Virgins 121
The Parable of the Talents 122
The Day and Hour Unknown 123

Chapter 13 – Wednesday & Thursday **125**
The Jews Plot to Kill Jesus 125
Jesus' Disciples Prepare for the Passover 125
Jesus Washes His Disciples' Feet 126
Jesus Predicts His Betrayal 126
Jesus Institutes Communion 127
Jesus Predicts Peter's Denial 128
Jesus Comforts His Disciples 128
Jesus Is the True Vine 130
The Hatred of the World 130
The Holy Spirit's Role 131
The Disciples' Grief Will Turn to Joy 131
Jesus Prays for Himself 132
Jesus Prays for His Disciples 132
Jesus Prays for All Believers 133
Jesus Prays on the Mount of Olives 133
Judas Betrays Jesus With a Kiss 134
Peter Cuts Off Malchus' Ear 135
Jesus Is Arrested 135
Annas Questions Jesus 135
Peter Denies Jesus 136

Chapter 14 – Friday & Saturday **137**
Jesus Stands Trial Before the Sanhedrin 137
Judas Hangs Himself 138
Jesus Stands Trial Before Pilate 138
Pilate Sends Jesus to Herod 139
Pilate Tries to Release Jesus 139
Pilate Sentences Jesus to Death 141
Simon of Cyrene Carries Jesus' Cross 141
Women Mourn for Jesus 141
Jesus Is Crucified 142
The Soldiers Cast Lots for Jesus' Clothing 142
Pilate Hangs a Sign on Jesus' Cross 142
The Crowd Insults Jesus 142
Jesus Saves the Repentant Criminal 143

Jesus Entrusts His Mother to John. 143
Jesus Gives Up His Spirit. 143
Supernatural Events Occur After Jesus' Death 143
Jesus' Friends and Family Mourn. 144
Jesus' Side Is Pierced. 144
Joseph of Arimathea and Nicodemus Claim Jesus' Body. 144
Soldiers Guard the Tomb 145

PART VI – ASCENSION **146**

CHAPTER 15 – Resurrection Sunday **147**
The Women Visit Jesus' Tomb 147
The Guards Report the Empty Tomb 148
Peter and John Race to the Tomb. 148
Jesus Appears to Mary Magdalene and Other Women 148
Jesus Appears to Two Disciples on the Road to Emmaus. 149
Jesus Appears to His Apostles 150

CHAPTER 16 – Jesus' Farewell to His Disciples **151**
Jesus Appears to Thomas 151
The Great Catch of Fish on the Sea of Galilee. 151
Jesus Restores Peter. 152
Jesus Gives the Great Commission 153
Jesus Ascends to Heaven. 153

EPILOGUE – That You May Believe and Have Life **155**
About C. Austin Tucker. **157**

Scripture Index

Matthew (MT)	
Scripture	Page
1:1-17	2
1:18-25a	10
1:25b	11
2:1-12	12
2:13-14	12
2:15	13
2:16-18	12
2:19-23	13
3:1-12	15
3:13-17	16
4:1-11	16
4:12	22
4:13-16	26
4:17	25
4:18-22	26
4:23-25	28
5:1	34
5:1-12	35
5:13	35
5:14-16	36
5:17-20	36
5:21-26	36
5:27-30	37
5:31-32	95
5:33-37	37
5:38-48	37
6:1-4	38
6:5-15	67
6:16-18	38
6:19-21	38
6:22-23	36
6:24	38
6:25-34	38
7:1-6	39

Matthew (MT)	
Scripture	Page
7:7-11	67
7:12	37
7:13-14	40
7:15-20	39
7:21-23	40
7:24-29	40
8:1-4	28
8:5-10	41
8:11-12	40
8:13	41
8:14-17	28
8:18	51
8:19-22	69
8:23-27	51
8:28-34	51
9:1	52
9:2-8	29
9:9-13	30
9:14-17	30
9:18-26	52
9:27-31	44
9:32-34	45
9:35	53
9:36	56
9:37-38	53
10:1	53
10:1-4	34
10:5-33	53
10:34-36	120
10:37-42	53
11:1	53
11:2-19	42
11:20-30	43
12:1-14	33

Matthew (MT)	
Scripture	Page
12:15-21	34
12:22-37	45
12:38-42	46
12:43-45	45
12:46-50	46
13:1-9	47
13:10-17	49
13:18-23	47
13:24-30	49
13:31-33	48
13:34-35	49
13:36a	49
13:36b-43	50
13:44-46	48
13:47-50	48
13:51-53	50
13:53-58	26
14:1-2	60
14:3-4	22
14:5-12	55
14:13-23	56
14:24-36	57
15:1-20	60
15:21-30	61
15:31	62
15:32-38	62
15:39	62
16:1-4	62
16:5-12	63
16:13-20	63
16:21-28	64
17:1-8	65
17:9-13	65
17:14-21	66

Matthew (MT)	
Scripture	**Page**
17:22-23	68
17:24-27	68
18:1-4	99
18:5-7	96
18:8-9	37
18:10-14	87
18:15-22	92
18:23-35	91
19:1-12	95
19:13-15	96
19:16-30	97
20:1-16	98
20:17-19	98
20:20-24	99
20:25-28	99
20:29-34	100
21:1-11	106
21:12-13	107
21:14-17	106
21:18-19	107
21:20-22	111
21:23-27	111
21:28-32	112
21:33-44	112
21:45-46	115
22:1-14	113
22:15-22	115
22:23-33	116
22:34-40	116
22:41-46	117
23:1-24	114
23:25-28	79
23:29-36	114
24:1-27	118
24:28	123
24:29-35	118

Matthew (MT)	
Scripture	**Page**
24:36-51	123
25:1-13	121
25:14-30	122
25:31-46	120
26:1-5	125
26:6-13	105
26:14-16	125
26:17-20	125
26:21-25	126
26:26-29	127
26:30	128
26:31-35	128
26:36-46	133
26:47-50a	134
26:50b-54	135
26:55-56	135
26:57	137
26:58a	135
26:58b	136
26:59-68	137
26:69-75	136
27:1-2	138
27:3-10	138
27:11-14	138
27:15-23	139
27:24-26	141
27:27-30	139
27:31-32	141
27:33-34	142
27:35-36	142
27:37	142
27:38	142
27:39-43	142
27:44	143
27:45-50	143
27:51-54	143

Matthew (MT)	
Scripture	**Page**
27:55-56	144
27:57-61	144
27:62-66	145
28:1-8	147
28:9-10	148
28:11-15	148
28:16-20a	153
28:20b	153

Mark (MK)	
Scripture	**Page**
1:1	1
1:2-8	15
1:9-11	16
1:12-13	16
1:14a	22
1:14b-15	25
1:16-20	26
1:21-28	27
1:29-34	28
1:35-38	28
1:39	28
1:40-45	28
2:1-12	29
2:13	30
2:14a	34
2:14b	30
2:15-17	30
2:18-22	30
2:23-28	33
3:1-6	33
3:7-12	34
3:13-19	34
3:20-21	46
3:22-30	45
3:31-35	46

Mark (MK)	
Scripture	Page
4:1-9	47
4:10-12	49
4:13-20	47
4:21-23	36
4:24	39
4:25	49
4:26-30	48
4:31-32	48
4:33-34	49
4:35-41	51
5:1-20	51
5:21-43	52
6:1-6a	26
6:6b-13	53
6:14-16	60
6:17	22
6:18-29	55
6:30-46	56
6:47-56	57
7:1-23	60
7:24-31	61
7:32-37	62
8:1-9a	62
8:9b-13	62
8:14-21	63
8:22-26	63
8:27-30	63
8:31-38	64
9:1	64
9:2-8	65
9:9-13	65
9:14-29	66
9:30-32	68
9:33a	68
9:33b-36	99
9:37	96

Mark (MK)	
Scripture	Page
9:38-41	56
9:42	96
9:43-49	37
9:50	35
10:1-12	95
10:13-16	96
10:17-31	97
10:32-34	98
10:35-41	99
10:42-45	99
10:46-52	100
11:1-11	106
11:12-18	107
11:19	106
11:20-24	111
11:25-26	67
11:27-33	111
12:1-11	112
12:12-17	115
12:18-27	116
12:28-34a	116
12:34b-37	117
12:38-40	114
12:41-44	117
13:1-31	118
13:32-37	123
14:1-2	125
14:3-9	105
14:10-11	125
14:12-17	125
14:18-21	126
14:22-25	127
14:26	128
14:27-31	128
14:32-42	133
14:43-45	134

Mark (MK)	
Scripture	Page
14:46a	135
14:46b	135
14:47	135
14:48-52	135
14:53	137
14:54a	135
14:54b	136
14:55-65	137
14:66-72	136
15:1-5	138
15:6-14	139
15:15	141
15:16-19	139
15:20-21	141
15:22-23	142
15:24	142
15:25	142
15:26	142
15:27-28	142
15:29-32a	142
15:32b	143
15:33-37	143
15:38-39	143
15:40-41	144
15:42-47	144
16:1-8	147
16:9	148
16:9a	155
16:9b	44
16:10	148
16:11	148
16:12-13	149
16:14	150
16:15-18	153
16:19a	153
16:19b-20	155

Luke (LK)	
Scripture	Page
1:1-4	1
1:5-25	7
1:26	8
1:27a	10
1:27b-38	8
1:39-45	8
1:46-56	9
1:57-66	9
1:67-80	9
2:1-7	10
2:8-20	11
2:21-38	11
2:39	13
2:40-52	13
3:1-18	15
3:19-20	22
3:21-22	16
3:23a	16
3:23b-38	3
4:1-13	16
4:14-15	25
4:16-30	26
4:31-37	27
4:38-41	28
4:42-43	28
4:44	28
5:1-11	26
5:12-16	28
5:17-26	29
5:27-32	30
5:33-39	30
6:1-11	33
6:12-16	34
6:17-19	34
6:20-26	35
6:27-36	37

Luke (LK)	
Scripture	Page
6:37-38	39
6:39	60
6:40	53
6:41-42	39
6:43-45	39
6:46-49	40
7:1-10	41
7:11-17	41
7:18-35	42
7:36-50	43
8:1-3	44
8:4-9	47
8:10	49
8:11-15	47
8:16-17	36
8:18	49
8:19-21	46
8:22-25	51
8:26-39	51
8:40-56	52
9:1-6	53
9:7-9	60
9:10-17	56
9:18-21	63
9:22-27	64
9:28-36a	65
9:36b	65
9:37-43a	66
9:43b-45	68
9:46-48	99
9:49-50	56
9:51-56	69
9:57-62	69
10:1	78
10:2-12	53
10:13-16	43

Luke (LK)	
Scripture	Page
10:17-20	78
10:21-24	43
10:25-37	78
10:38-42	79
11:1-13	67
11:14-15	45
11:16	46
11:17-26	45
11:27-32	46
11:33-36	36
11:37-41	79
11:42-43	114
11:44	79
11:45	114
11:47-52	114
11:53-54	115
12:1a	62
12:1b	63
12:2-9	53
12:10	45
12:11-12	53
12:13-21	80
12:22-31	38
12:32-34	38
12:35-48	123
12:49-53	120
12:54-56	62
13:1-9	80
13:10-17	81
13:18-21	48
13:22	95
13:23-30	40
13:31-33	85
13:34-35	106
14:1-6	85
14:7-14	86

Luke (LK)	
Scripture	Page
14:15-24	86
14:25-33	87
14:34-35	35
15:1-7	87
15:8-10	88
15:11-32	88
16:1-16	89
16:17	36
16:18	95
16:19-31	90
17:1-3	96
17:3-4	92
17:5-6	66
17:7-10	92
17:11-19	95
17:20-21	90
17:22-25	118
17:26-37	123
18:1-8	68
18:9-14	117
18:15-17	96
18:18-30	97
18:31-34	98
18:35-43	100
19:1-10	100
19:11-28	101
19:29-44	106
19:45-46	107
19:47-48	108
20:1-8	111
20:9-18	112
20:19-26	115
20:27-39	116
20:40-44	117
20:45-47	114
21:1-4	117

Luke (LK)	
Scripture	Page
21:5-33	118
21:34-35	120
21:36-38	123
22:1-6	125
22:7-14	125
22:15-20	127
22:21-23	126
22:24-30	99
22:31-34	128
22:35-39	128
22:40-46	133
22:47-48	134
22:49-51	135
22:52-53	135
22:54	135
22:55-62	136
22:63-71	137
23:1-5	138
23:6-12	139
23:13-22	139
23:23-25	141
23:26	141
23:27-31	141
23:32-34a	142
23:34b	142
23:35	142
23:36-37	143
23:38	142
23:39-43	143
23:44-45a	143
23:45b	143
23:46	143
23:47	143
23:48-49	144
23:50-56	144
24:1-8	147

Luke (LK)	
Scripture	Page
24:9	148
24:10	147
24:11-12	148
24:13-35	149
24:36-43	150
24:44-53	153

John (JN)	
Scripture	Page
1:1-18	1
1:19-28	17
1:29-34	18
1:35-42	18
1:43-51	18
1:45a	34
2:1-12	19
2:13-25	19
3:1-21	20
3:22-23	21
3:24	22
3:25-36	21
4:1-2	21
4:3	22
4:4-26	22
4:27-38	23
4:39-43	23
4:44	26
4:45	25
4:46-54	25
5:1-15	30
5:16-47	31
6:1-15	56
6:16-24	57
6:25-59	58
6:60-71	59
7:1	59

John (JN)	
Scripture	Page
7:2-9	69
7:10	69
7:11-24	71
7:25-44	72
7:45-52	75
7:53	73
8:1	73
8:2-11	75
8:12-29	73
8:30-59	73
9:1-41	76
10:1-21	77
10:22-39	81
10:40-42	85
11:1	93
11:2	105
11:3-44	93
11:16a	34
11:45-54	95
11:55-57	102
12:1-8	105
12:9-11	102
12:12-19	106
12:20-50	108
13:1-17	126
13:18-30	126
13:31-32	127
13:33-38	128
14:1-31	128
15:1-17	130
15:18-27	130
16:1-4	130
16:5-15	131
16:16-33	131
17:1-5	132
17:6-19	132

John (JN)	
Scripture	Page
17:20-26	133
18:1	133
18:2-9	134
18:10-11	135
18:12	135
18:13-16	135
18:17-18	136
18:19-23	135
18:24	137
18:25-27	136
18:28-38	138
18:39-40	139
19:1-15	139
19:16a	141
19:16b-17a	141
19:17b-18	142
19:19-22	142
19:23-24	142
19:25a	143
19:25b	144
19:26-27	143
19:28-30	143
19:31-37	144
19:38-42	144
20:1	147
20:2-9	148
20:10-18	148
20:19-23	150
20:24-29	151
20:30-31	155
21:1-14	151
21:15-23	152
21:24-25	155

Acts	
Scripture	Page
1:3	155
1:4-12	153
1:18-19	138

1 Corinthians (1 COR)	
Scripture	Page
11:25-26	127
15:5-7	155
15:6a	153

Introduction to The Chronological Word Truth Life Bible

The Chronological Word Truth Life Bible is published by Route 66 Ministries, which is so named in reference to the 66 books of the Bible. The ministry is dedicated to teaching people to encounter God through reading and understanding the Bible in chronological order.

Two scriptures in the Gospel of John inspired the "Word Truth Life" series title. John the disciple identifies Jesus as the **Word** (John 1:1, John 1:14), and Jesus identified himself as the Way, the **Truth**, and the **Life** (John 14:6). These adjectives not only apply to Jesus himself, but to the book that illuminates him, the Bible.

The Word Truth Life Bible (WTLB) was born of the desire to provide a Bible version that's easier to read and understand. Many Christians know the Bible's familiar stories, but for many reasons they don't read the entire Bible to learn how everything fits together. Some of the most common reasons for this are:

* The Bible is big.
* The Bible is confusing.
* The Bible is boring.

The WTLB solves these issues. Although there will be many differences in comparison with traditional Bibles, Route 66 Ministries is committed not only to acknowledging the full and complete authority of scripture, but also remaining true to its entire message. Therefore, despite its different packaging, unique formatting, and shorter length, none of the Bible's content is missing. This has been the main concern in undertaking such a project.

Here are just a few benefits of The Word Truth Life Bible:

It's chronological – Events are placed in the order that they occurred, as far as could be determined.

It's harmonized – Harmonization is one of the main features that makes this Bible unique. It means scriptures that provide the same information are merged into one narrative. Most people are familiar with harmonies of the Gospels, but once this Bible is complete, it will harmonize scripture from Genesis to Revelation.

It's shorter – Because of the harmonization feature, the entire Bible is shorter, but no information is lost. This eliminates the intimidation of reading such a huge book. For example, all four Gospels can be read in half the time it would normally take.

It's uniquely formatted – For example:

* Chapters and verses have been removed from within the narratives to prevent unnatural breaks in the story line. However, scripture references are present in the heading of each section for those who prefer them.

* Scripture references are aligned right instead of left; this makes it easier to read the Bible like a novel, as the headings don't interfere with or interrupt the reading flow.

* Tables and bullets are used to break up text, making the information easier to understand.

* Dialogue is formatted as is common in novels, making it easier to follow the speaker.

Because of the vastness of such a project, each portion of the Bible is being published as it is completed. Old Testament volumes will continue to be published in the coming year, as well as Acts in the New Testament.

Connect with us to follow the publication progress of future installments and receive Bible-reading tips:

Website: Route66Ministries.com

Facebook: Facebook.com/Route66Ministries

Twitter: Twitter.com/ReadtheBibleR66

We look forward to accompanying you on this journey as you experience the Bible in a new and exciting way. And please let us know what you think. You can ask questions about this translation or report errors or concerns by emailing *wtlb@wordtruthlifebible.com*.

KJV, NIV, ESV – A Word
About Bible Translations

Walk into any Christian bookstore and you'll find countless Bibles in various translations and for different groups of people. What exactly does translation mean? It's simply the process of taking words from one language and expressing them in a different language. So American Bibles translate the original Hebrew, Aramaic, and Greek texts into English. Many people view multiple translations as a bad thing, but translations aren't evil; they're necessary. Without them, only people who know the original languages could read the Bible, but God intended that all people be able to read and understand its riches.

But why so many translations? Because of the complexity of language, one can write a concept or phrase in many different ways; there's more than one way to skin a cat! (Notice how those last two sentences state the same thing in two completely different ways.)

Some people choose certain translations based on how well they understand them, some choose based on the beauty and style of the language, while others choose based on word-for-word translation accuracy. All translations have their benefits, and there's no need to choose sides. Everyone is entitled to his preference. Each Bible translation serves a different function, depending on your purpose for reading it.

The King James Version

Many of us grew up reading the King James Version (KJV), and it remains one of the most beautiful translations ever penned. It's truly a literary masterpiece! Now, the KJV is also known as the "authorized version," but that title doesn't make it superior to other Bibles. It simply means that King James of England authorized its publication. But many people believe that the KJV is the only true Bible translation and that all other translations "change" the true word of God. This simply isn't true.

Despite the beauty of the old English language, the KJV isn't as accurate as more modern translations like the English Standard Version (ESV) or the New International Version (NIV). The reason for this has to do with the source text used for translation.

Here's an overview: The term "manuscripts" refers to the Greek and Hebrew documents containing the text of the Bible. Now the manuscripts available when the KJV was published were flawed, and knowledge of the languages — particularly Hebrew — was not as advanced as it is today. The scholars did an excellent job with what they had. However, more accurate manuscripts were found after the KJV was published, and subsequent Bible translations use them as their underlying text. So that's the reason for the differences between the KJV and other translations. No conspiracy involved! :-)

Because we speak English, it's easy to forget that we don't have a monopoly on the perfect Bible translation. People in other countries need to read the Bible too. So there are German translations, Spanish translations, Italian translations, etc. No single translation is inspired in the same way the original documents were; therefore none deserves to be put on a pedestal to the exclusion of the others.

It's fine to embrace our own traditions but it's not fair to insist that everyone else embrace them too. Many translations were published before the KJV, many were published afterward, and many will be published in the future. Instead of making the KJV the standard by which all other translations are judged, we must evaluate it along with every other translation to determine whether it most accurately reflects the author's intent and meaning as written in the original language.

Reading the KJV today is difficult simply because we don't speak the way they spoke back then. There's a barrier between our language and theirs. The people who lived in the 1600s spoke the same English in which the KJV was written, but we don't speak the King's English anymore. As language changes and words take on different meanings, new translations are necessary. Just as they had a Bible in the 1600s that reflected the way they actually spoke, people today need the same. It's not necessary to struggle over archaic words meant for a different time when translations with more modern phrasing are available.

The Word Truth Life Bible is different from other Bibles because of its goal: To provide a Bible that will aid people in reading and understanding all that God has to say, without the hindrances of the traditional Bible format.

The Bible's message remains intact — no content is missing. All stories include the same details that were originally present. The WTLB is not intended to take the place of traditional Bibles, which will always be necessary for use in church services and for in-depth Bible study. Nor is this Bible intended to replace your favorite translation. Everyone should have multiple translations available for different tasks and for the insight gained in noting the differences between them. This Bible is simply an addition to your library. It's for reading the Bible like a novel and gaining a true understanding of its overall story. It's perfect for those new to the Bible, those who want to introduce others to the Bible, and those who simply want a fresh new way to read it.

Behold The Lamb:
An Introduction to This Book

"Who do you say that I am?" Jesus asked that question of his disciples in Matthew 16:15 and since that time, the question has been asked throughout the centuries. Is he Messiah, man, or myth? Lord, liar, or lunatic? God, guru, or genie?

Theories abound, and each year documentaries try to discover the "truth." But the best place to find answers is in the Gospels themselves. God has revealed himself through nature and through history, but the ultimate revelation of himself comes through knowledge of his Son, Jesus Christ.

Each of the four Gospels — Matthew, Mark, Luke, and John — covers Jesus' time on earth from its own unique perspective. They don't contradict each other, but they provide puzzle pieces of Jesus' life that fit together beautifully to form a complete picture. Reformed scholar Martin Luther once said, "We have four evangelists, and [al]though four books labeled 'Gospel' appear in the Bible, we have only one Gospel. One message presented from four different, complementary points of view."

Attempting to merge the Gospels into one compelling story is truly a humbling endeavor. Not all of the Gospels are in chronological order, and if some of them are, we don't know which ones. Therefore we can only guess about the chronology. Nevertheless, trying to determine the order of events and piecing them together is the joy of those who attempt to harmonize the Gospels.

It's essential to understand that it's not as important **when** events occurred, only that they **did** occur. This Gospel harmony seeks to provide a possible sequence of events, without omitting any of the information that each Gospel uniquely provides. But it doesn't presume to be the final authority— it is only one interpretation among many. It's not meant to be a replacement for reading and studying the Gospels in full for yourself.

I invite you to Explore the Word, Embrace the Truth, and Experience Life!

C. Austin Tucker

PART I
JESUS' EARLY YEARS

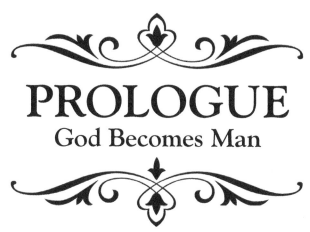

PROLOGUE
God Becomes Man

Introduction
MK 1:1|LK 1:1-4

This is the beginning of the good news about Jesus Christ, the Son of God.

Most excellent Theophilus, as you know, certain events have been fulfilled among us. They were conveyed to us by eyewitnesses and ministers of the Gospel who saw these things from the very beginning. Since others have written about these events, I decided to write an orderly account for you, carefully investigating everything from the very beginning, so that you can be sure of the things you've been taught.

The Word Becomes Flesh
JN 1:1-18

In the beginning, the Word existed; he was with God from the very beginning. Now the Word was with God and the Word was God — all things were made through him and nothing would exist without him. In him was life and that life was the light of men. The light shines in the darkness, but the darkness does not understand it.

God sent a man named John as a witness to testify about that light, so all men could believe through him. He testified about Jesus, saying, "This is the one I told you about. He came after me, but he's greater than me because he existed before me." John himself wasn't the light — he came only as a witness to tell everyone that the true light who gives light to everyone was coming into the world.

The Word was in the world but even though the world was made through him, the world didn't recognize him. He came to his own people but they didn't receive him. But he gave to everyone who received him and believed in his name the right to become children of God. These children

1

weren't born because a human planned it or a husband desired it. Theirs wasn't a physical birth; instead, they were born of God.

The Word became flesh and lived among us. We saw the glory of the One and Only, who came from the Father, full of grace and truth. Because of the fullness of his grace, we all received one blessing after another, for the law was given through Moses, but grace and truth came through Jesus Christ. No one has ever seen God except the Unique One, who is also God and sits at the Father's side. He has made God known.

Jesus' Genealogy Through Joseph
MT 1:1-17

This is the genealogy of Jesus Christ, a descendant of David and of Abraham:

Abraham was the father of Isaac.
Isaac was the father of Jacob.
Jacob was the father of Judah and his brothers.

Judah was the father of Perez and
Zerah (whose mother was Tamar).
Perez was the father of Hezron.
Hezron was the father of Ram.

Ram was the father of Amminadab.
Amminadab was the father of Nahshon.
Nahshon was the father of Salmon.

Salmon was the father of Boaz
(whose mother was Rahab).
Boaz was the father of Obed (whose mother was Ruth).
Obed was the father of Jesse.

Jesse was the father of King David.
David was the father of Solomon
(whose mother was Bathsheba, Uriah's widow).

Solomon was the father of Rehoboam.
Rehoboam was the father of Abijah.
Abijah was the father of Asa.

Asa was the father of Jehoshaphat.
Jehoshaphat was the father of Jehoram.
Jehoram was the father of Uzziah.

Uzziah was the father of Jotham.
Jotham was the father of Ahaz.
Ahaz was the father of Hezekiah.

Hezekiah was the father of Manasseh.
Manasseh was the father of Amon.
Amon was the father of Josiah.

Josiah was the father of Jehoiachin
and his brothers (born during the Babylonian exile).
After the Babylonian exile:
Jehoiachin was the father of Shealtiel.
Shealtiel was the father of Zerubbabel.

Zerubbabel was the father of Abiud.
Abiud was the father of Eliakim.
Eliakim was the father of Azor.

Azor was the father of Zadok.
Zadok was the father of Akim.
Akim was the father of Eliud.

Eliud was the father of Eleazar.
Eleazar was the father of Matthan.
Matthan was the father of Jacob.

Jacob was the father of Joseph, Mary's husband. She gave birth to Jesus, who is called the Christ.

These include 14 generations from Abraham to David, 14 from David to the Babylonian exile, and 14 from the Babylonian exile to the birth of Christ.

Jesus' Genealogy Through Mary
LK 3:23b-38

Jesus (who was thought to be the son of Joseph) was the [grand]son of Heli,

the son of Matthat,
the son of Levi,
the son of Melki,
the son of Jannai,
the son of Joseph,

3

the son of Mattathias,
the son of Amos,
the son of Nahum,
the son of Esli,
the son of Naggai,

the son of Maath,
the son of Mattathias,
the son of Semein,
the son of Josech,
the son of Joda,

the son of Joanan,
the son of Rhesa,
the son of Zerubbabel,
the son of Shealtiel,
the son of Neri,

the son of Melki,
the son of Addi,
the son of Cosam,
the son of Elmadam,
the son of Er,

the son of Joshua,
the son of Eliezer,
the son of Jorim,
the son of Matthat,
the son of Levi,

the son of Simeon,
the son of Judah,
the son of Joseph,
the son of Jonam,
the son of Eliakim,

the son of Melea,
the son of Menna,
the son of Mattatha,
the son of Nathan,
the son of David,

the son of Jesse,
the son of Obed,
the son of Boaz,
the son of Salmon,
the son of Nahshon,

the son of Amminadab,
the son of Admin,
the son of Arni,
the son of Hezron,
the son of Perez,

the son of Judah,
the son of Jacob,
the son of Isaac,
the son of Abraham,
the son of Terah,

the son of Nahor,
the son of Serug,
the son of Reu,
the son of Peleg,
the son of Eber,

the son of Shelah,
the son of Cainan,
the son of Arphaxad,
the son of Shem,
the son of Noah,

the son of Lamech,
the son of Methuselah,
the son of Enoch,
the son of Jared,
the son of Mahalalel,

the son of Kenan,
the son of Enosh,
the son of Seth,
the son of Adam,
the son of God.

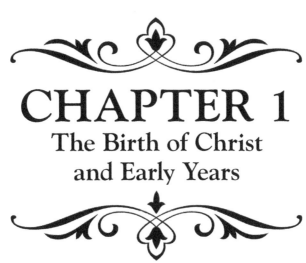

CHAPTER 1
The Birth of Christ
and Early Years

The Angel Gabriel Predicts John the Baptist's Birth
LK 1:5-25

When Herod was king of Judea, there lived a priest named Zechariah who belonged to the priestly division of Abijah. His wife Elizabeth was also a descendant of Aaron. God considered them both righteous because they observed all his commandments and requirements blamelessly. But they had no children because they were both very old and Elizabeth was unable to conceive.

Zechariah's priestly division was on duty. One day, according to their custom, the priests drew lots to determine their responsibilities, and Zechariah was chosen to burn incense in the Lord's temple. At the appointed time, the people assembled outside and prayed.

An angel of the Lord suddenly appeared at the right side of the altar of incense, and Zechariah was surprised and terrified.

"Don't be afraid, Zechariah," the angel said. "God has heard your prayer and Elizabeth will give birth to a son. You must name him John. Many will rejoice when he is born, and he'll be a joy and a delight to you. He will be filled with the Holy Spirit even from birth and will be great in the Lord's sight. He should never drink wine or beer. He will bring many Israelites back to the Lord their God, preparing the way for the Lord in the spirit and power of Elijah — to turn the hearts of the fathers to their children and the disobedient to the wisdom of the righteous — to make ready a people prepared for the Lord."

"How can I be sure this will happen?" Zechariah asked. "My wife and I are very old."

"I am Gabriel," the angel said. "I stand in God's presence and I've been sent to tell you this good news. But since you didn't believe me, you won't be able to speak until your son is born, which will come to pass at the proper time."

The people waiting outside wondered why Zechariah stayed in the temple so long. When he came out, he couldn't speak but kept making signs to them, so they realized he had seen a vision.

Then Zechariah returned home. Later, Elizabeth got pregnant and praised God, saying, "The Lord has shown me favor and taken away my disgrace among the people."

And she remained in seclusion for five months.

Gabriel Predicts Jesus' Birth
LK 1:26|LK 1:27b-38

Then God sent the angel Gabriel to Nazareth, a city in Galilee, where he visited a virgin named Mary. "Greetings," he said, "you are highly favored and the Lord is with you."

Mary was troubled and wondered why he greeted her this way.

"Don't be afraid," Gabriel said. "You've found favor with God. You will give birth to a son and you must name him Jesus. He will be great and will be called the Son of the Most High. The Lord God will give him the throne of his father David, and he'll reign over the house of Jacob forever; his kingdom will never end."

"I'm a virgin," Mary said. "How will this happen?"

"The Holy Spirit will come upon you and the power of the Most High will overshadow you. Therefore the Holy One born to you will be called the Son of God. Even your relative Elizabeth, who was said to be barren, is going to have a child in her old age. She's six months pregnant. So you see, nothing is impossible with God."

"I am the Lord's servant," Mary replied. "May everything happen just as you said."

Then the angel left.

Mary Visits Elizabeth
LK 1:39-45

Afterward, Mary prepared herself and rushed to a city in the hill country of Judea to see Elizabeth and Zechariah. As soon as Mary greeted her, Elizabeth's baby leaped in her womb.

Elizabeth was filled with the Holy Spirit and exclaimed, "You are blessed among women, and so is the child you will bear! But why am I so favored that the mother of my Lord visits me? My baby immediately leaped for joy at the sound of your voice. You are blessed because you believe that the Lord's promise will be fulfilled!"

Then Mary sang:

"My soul glorifies the Lord and my spirit rejoices in God my Savior because he has favored me, his humble servant. From now on all generations will call me blessed because the Mighty One has done great things for me, and his name is holy.

"He extends mercy to those who honor him, from generation to generation. He performed mighty deeds with his arm and scattered those who are filled with pride. He brought down rulers from their thrones but lifted up the humble.

"He filled the hungry with good things but sent the rich away empty-handed. He helped his servant Israel, remembering to be merciful to Abraham and his descendants forever, just as he promised our ancestors."

Mary stayed with Elizabeth for about three months and then returned home.

When Elizabeth gave birth to her son, her neighbors and relatives rejoiced with her because the Lord had shown her great mercy.

They circumcised the child on the eighth day and were going to name him Zechariah, after his father, but Elizabeth said, "No! We must name him John."

"But none of your relatives are named John," they replied.

They motioned to Zechariah to find out what he wanted to name the child. So he asked for a writing tablet and wrote, *His name is John.*

And everyone was amazed.

Immediately Zechariah's mouth was opened and his tongue was set free, and he began to praise God.

The people were astonished and went throughout the hill country of Judea talking about everything that had happened. Everyone who heard about it was amazed and asked, "What kind of person will this child become?" For the Lord was certainly with him.

Zechariah was filled with the Holy Spirit and prophesied: "Praise the Lord, the God of Israel, because he has redeemed his people. He raised up a horn of salvation for us in the house of his servant David — as he promised through his holy prophets long ago — salvation from our enemies and from the clutches of all who hate us.

"He showed mercy to our fathers and remembered his holy covenant — the promise he made to our father Abraham. He rescued us from the clutches of our enemies, enabling us to serve him without fear — in holiness and righteousness in his presence forever.

"And you, my child, will be called a prophet of the Most High, because you will go before the Lord to prepare the way for him — to give his people the knowledge of salvation through the forgiveness of their sins.

"Because of our God's merciful compassion, the rising sun will visit us from heaven and shine on those living in darkness and in the shadow of death, to guide our feet to the path of peace."

John grew up and became spiritually strong. He lived in the desert until he appeared publicly to Israel.

An Angel Appears to Joseph
MT 1:18-25a|LK 1:27a

Now this is how the birth of Jesus the Messiah came about. Mary was engaged to a man named Joseph — a descendant of David — but she became pregnant by the Holy Spirit before they got married. So Joseph decided to legally end the engagement. But he was a righteous man and didn't want to disgrace her publicly, so he decided to end it privately.

But an angel of the Lord appeared to him in a dream and said, "Joseph, son of David, don't be afraid to take Mary as your wife, because the baby within her is from the Holy Spirit. She will have a son you will name Jesus, because he will save his people from their sins."

This fulfilled what the Lord said through the prophet, *The virgin will conceive and give birth to a son, and they will call him Immanuel* — which means, "God with us."

When Joseph woke up, he obeyed the angel of the Lord and took Mary as his wife, but they didn't consummate the marriage until she gave birth.

Jesus Christ Is Born
LK 2:1-7

During this time, Caesar Augustus ordered that a census be taken of the entire Roman world — this was the first census that took place while Quirinius was governor of Syria. So the people went to their hometown to register.

Since Joseph was a descendant of David, he and Mary left Nazareth and went to Judea to register in Bethlehem — the city of David. Mary gave birth to her firstborn son while they were there. She wrapped him in cloths and laid him in a manger, because there was no room for them at the inn.

An Angel Announces Jesus' Birth to Shepherds
LK 2:8-20

Now shepherds were living in the fields nearby, watching over their flocks that night. An angel of the Lord appeared and the glory of the Lord blazed around them. They were terrified!

"Don't be afraid," the angel said. "I have good news that will bring great joy for all people. Today your Savior has been born in the city of David; he is Christ, the Lord. This is how you can identify him: he will be wrapped in cloths and lying in a manger."

Suddenly the angel was joined by a large number of heavenly host, and they praised God, saying, "Glory to God in heaven; peace on earth to those with whom he is pleased."

After the angels returned to heaven, the shepherds said, "Let's go to Bethlehem and find the child the Lord told us about."

So they hurried off. They found Mary and Joseph, and saw the baby lying in a manger. Then the shepherds went and shared what they had been told about the child, and everyone was amazed. The shepherds returned to the fields, glorifying and praising God for everything they had seen and heard, which had taken place just as they had been told.

Mary stored these things in her heart and often thought about them.

Jesus' Parents Present Him at the Temple
MT 1:25b|LK 2:21-38

Eight days later Mary and Joseph circumcised the baby and named him Jesus, the name the angel had given him before he was conceived. When it was time for the purification ritual required by the Law of Moses, they went to Jerusalem. There they presented Jesus to the Lord — as it is written in the Law of the Lord, *Every firstborn male must be consecrated to the Lord.* And they offered a sacrifice for their purification: *two doves or two young pigeons.*

A righteous and dedicated man named Simeon lived in Jerusalem, and he was waiting for God to end Israel's distress. The Holy Spirit was upon him and had revealed to him that he would see the Lord's Messiah before he died, so the Spirit led him into the temple courts.

When Mary and Joseph arrived to dedicate Jesus, Simeon held the child and praised God, saying, "Sovereign Lord, now you dismiss your servant in peace, just as you promised. For I have now seen with my own eyes your salvation, which you prepared for all people — he will bring the light of revelation to the Gentiles and glory to your people Israel."

Mary and Joseph were amazed!

Simeon blessed them and said to Mary, "This child is destined to cause the humbling and exaltation of many in Israel. He will be a sign that will generate opposition among many people, so that their innermost thoughts about him will be exposed. And a sword will pierce your own soul too."

A prophetess named Anna was also there. Her father was Penuel from the tribe of Asher. She was very old. She had become a widow after being married for only 7 years and was still a widow at age 84. She worshiped in the temple night and day, fasting and praying. She approached Jesus and his parents and gave thanks to God, speaking about Jesus to everyone who was anticipating Jerusalem's redemption.

Wise Men Visit Jesus
MT 2:1-12

Some time later, during King Herod's reign and after Jesus' birth in Bethlehem, wise men from the east visited Jerusalem.

They asked, "Where is the one born king of the Jews? We saw his star rise in the east and came to worship him."

Their question concerned King Herod and all the people of Jerusalem, so Herod gathered the chief priests and teachers of the law and asked them where the Messiah was supposed to be born.

"In Bethlehem in Judea," they replied. "The prophet wrote: *Bethlehem, land of Judah, you are certainly not the least among the leading cities of Judah, for a ruler will come from you and shepherd my people Israel."*

Herod sent for the wise men secretly and found out the exact time the star had appeared. He sent them to Bethlehem, saying, "Search carefully for the child. Let me know as soon as you find him so I can go worship him too."

The wise men left, and the same star they had seen in the east guided them and stopped over the house where Jesus was, and they were overjoyed. They went in and found the child with his mother Mary, and they bowed down and worshiped him. They opened their treasures and gave him gifts of gold, frankincense, and myrrh.

They had been warned in a dream not to report back to Herod, so they returned to their country by another route.

Jesus' Family Escapes to Egypt
MT 2:13-14|MT 2:16-18

Then an angel of the Lord appeared to Joseph in a dream and said, "Get up and take your family to Egypt and stay there until further notice. Herod is planning to search for the child and kill him."

So they left for Egypt during the night.

Herod was furious when he realized that the wise men had tricked him. Based on the timing of Jesus' birth revealed by the wise men, he ordered the killing of all boys under two years old who lived in Bethlehem and its vicinity. This fulfilled what was said through the prophet Jeremiah: *A bitter cry is heard in Ramah, Rachel is weeping and mourning for her children and refusing to be comforted, because they are gone.*

Jesus' Family Returns to Nazareth
MT 2:15|MT 2:19-23|LK 2:39

Now Joseph was still in Egypt when Herod died. An angel of the Lord appeared to him in a dream and said, "Take your family to Israel. Those who were trying to kill the child are dead." This fulfilled what the Lord had said through the prophet, *I called my son out of Egypt.*

So Joseph did as he was told. But he was afraid to go to Judea because he had been warned that Herod's son Archelaus was the new ruler. So they returned to Galilee, to their hometown of Nazareth. This fulfilled what was said through the prophets, that he would be called a Nazarene.

Young Jesus Stays Behind in Jerusalem
LK 2:40-52

Every year Mary and Joseph went to Jerusalem for the Passover Feast, according to Jewish custom. On one such visit, Jesus was 12 years old. Afterward Mary and Joseph started home and traveled for a day, thinking Jesus was with them. They didn't know he had stayed behind in Jerusalem.

When they realized he wasn't with them, they searched for him among their relatives and friends and then returned to Jerusalem to look for him. They found him three days later in the temple courts, listening to the teachers and asking questions. His level of understanding and his answers to their questions surprised everyone, and his parents were amazed.

"Son, why did you treat us this way?" his mother asked. "Your father and I have been anxiously searching for you."

"Why were you searching for me?" Jesus asked. "Didn't you know I had to be in my Father's house?"

But they didn't understand what he meant.

So they returned to Nazareth and Jesus obeyed his parents, and Mary occasionally reflected on these events.

Jesus grew in stature and became strong, and he was filled with wisdom. God's grace was upon him and he found favor with God and men.

CHAPTER 2
The Beginning of Jesus' Ministry

John the Baptist Prepares the Way
MT 3:1-12|MK 1:2-8|LK 3:1-18

It was the 15th year of Emperor Tiberius Caesar's reign. Pontius Pilate was governor of Judea, Herod ruled Galilee, his brother Philip ruled Iturea and Traconitis, and Lysanias ruled Abilene. Annas and Caiaphas served as high priests.

At that time the word of God came to John, son of Zechariah, in the Desert of Judea. His clothes were made of camel's hair and he wore a leather belt around his waist. He ate locusts and wild honey. He went throughout the country around the Jordan and preached a baptism of repentance for the forgiveness of sins, saying, "Repent, for the kingdom of heaven is near."

This is what the prophets Malachi and Isaiah said: *I will send my messenger ahead of you, who will prepare the way for you. A voice of one calling out in the desert: Prepare the way for the Lord; make straight paths for him. Every valley will be filled in, every mountain and hill made low. The crooked roads will become straight, and the rough ways smooth. And all humanity will see God's salvation.*

People came from Jerusalem, Judea, and the region of the Jordan. They confessed their sins and John baptized them in the Jordan River.

When the Pharisees and Sadducees visited him there, John said, "You brood of vipers! Who warned you to flee from the coming wrath? Produce fruit that demonstrates repentance. It's not good enough to simply claim Abraham as your father, because God can raise up children for Abraham from these stones. The ax is already at the root of the trees, and every tree that doesn't produce good fruit will be cut down and thrown into the fire."

"What should we do?" the crowd asked.

John replied, "Anyone with two shirts should share with he who has none. Those with extra food should do the same."

Tax collectors came to be baptized and asked, "Teacher, what should we do?"

"Don't collect more money than required."

"And what should we do?" some soldiers asked.

"Don't extort money using threats or false accusations. Be satisfied with your pay."

The people were in a state of expectation, wondering whether John could be the Christ.

"I baptize you with water," John replied, "but someone more powerful is coming. I'm not even worthy to kneel, untie the thongs of his sandals, and carry them. He will baptize you with the Holy Spirit and with fire. His winnowing fork is in his hand to clear his threshing floor and gather the wheat into his barn, but the chaff he will burn up with unquenchable fire."

And John continued preaching the good news to them with many encouraging words.

John Baptizes Jesus
MT 3:13-17|MK 1:9-11|LK 3:21-22

While John was baptizing the people at the Jordan River, Jesus traveled there from Nazareth in Galilee to be baptized.

But John tried to stop him. "I need to be baptized by you," he said. "Why have you come to me?"

"Because it's necessary to fulfill all that God requires," Jesus replied.

So John consented.

Jesus was praying as he emerged from the water. Then he saw heaven tear open, and the Spirit of God descended in the form of a dove and rested upon him.

A voice from heaven said, "You are my Son, whom I love; I'm very pleased with you."

Satan Tempts Jesus in the Desert
MT 4:1-11|MK 1:12-13|LK 3:23a|LK 4:1-13

Now Jesus was about 30 years old when he began his ministry. He was filled with the Holy Spirit when he left the Jordan, and the Spirit led him into the desert to be tempted by the devil, Satan.

Wild animals surrounded Jesus, and Satan tempted him for 40 days and 40 nights. Jesus hadn't eaten anything during that time and at the end of the fast, he was hungry.

"If you're the Son of God," Satan said, "tell these stones to become bread."

Jesus answered, "It is written, *Man does not live by bread alone, but by every word that comes from the mouth of God.*"

Then Satan took Jesus to Jerusalem, the holy city, and had him stand on the highest point of the temple. "If you're the Son of God, throw yourself down from this place. For it is written: *He will command his angels to protect you* and *They will lift you up with their hands so that you won't strike your foot against a stone.*"

Jesus replied, "It is also written, *Do not test the Lord your God.*"

Satan took him up to a very high mountain and showed him in an instant all the kingdoms of the world. "I will give you all their splendor and all authority; it's been given to me and I can give it to anyone I wish. Bow down and worship me and it will all be yours."

"Get away from me, Satan! For it is written, *Worship the Lord your God and serve only him.*"

So the devil left him until a more suitable time. Then angels came and ministered to Jesus.

John Denies Being the Christ
JN 1:19-28

Some of the Jews in Jerusalem sent priests and Levites to ask John about his identity.

"I'm not the Messiah," John confessed.

"Who are you then? Are you Elijah?"

"No, I'm not."

"Are you the Prophet?"

"No."

"Tell us who you are so we can relay the information to those who sent us. What do you have to say about yourself?"

John replied in the words of Isaiah the prophet, "I'm *the voice of one calling in the desert, 'Make a straight path for the Lord to travel.'*"

Some Pharisees who had been sent asked, "If you aren't the Messiah, Elijah, or the Prophet, why do you baptize?"

"I baptize with water," John replied, "but there's someone among you whom you don't know. He will come after me, but I'm not worthy to untie even the straps of his sandals."

This happened at Bethany on the other side of the Jordan, where John was baptizing.

John Declares Jesus the Lamb of God
JN 1:29-34

The next day John saw Jesus walking toward him and said, "Look, the Lamb of God, who takes away the sin of the world! He's the one I meant when I said, 'The one who comes after me is greater than me, because he existed before me.'

"I didn't know who he was, but I baptized with water so that he would be revealed to Israel. I saw the Spirit descend from heaven as a dove and rest on him. He who sent me to baptize had told me, 'The man on whom you see the Spirit rest is the one who will baptize with the Holy Spirit.' I witnessed this and I testify that he is the Son of God."

John's Disciples Follow Jesus
JN 1:35-42

The next day John was standing there again, with two of his disciples. He saw Jesus passing by and said, "Look, the Lamb of God!"

So John's disciples followed Jesus.

Jesus turned around, saw them, and asked, "What do you want?"

"Rabbi, where are you staying?" (Rabbi means teacher.)

"Come and you will see."

So Jesus showed them where he was staying and they spent the day with him. It was about 4pm.

Andrew was one of John's disciples who had heard what John said and followed Jesus. The first thing he did was go tell his brother Simon, "We found the Messiah!" (Messiah means the Christ or anointed one.) Then he brought Simon to Jesus.

Jesus said, "You are Simon, son of John, but now you will be called Peter." (In Aramaic, Peter is translated *Cephas.*)

Philip and Nathanael Follow Jesus
JN 1:43-51

The next day Jesus decided to leave for Galilee. He found Philip and said, "Follow me."

Like Andrew and Peter, Philip was from Bethsaida. He went and told Nathanael, "We found the one Moses and the prophets wrote about – Jesus of Nazareth, the son of Joseph."

"Nazareth! Can anything good come from there?" Nathanael asked.

"Come and see," Philip said.

As Nathanael approached, Jesus said, "Here's a true Israelite in whom there is nothing false."

"How do you know me?" Nathanael asked.

"I saw you under the fig tree before Philip called you."

"Rabbi," Nathanael said, "you are the Son of God; you are the King of Israel."

"You believe because I said I saw you under the fig tree," Jesus said. "You will see greater things than that. I assure you, heaven will open and you will see the angels of God ascending and descending on the Son of Man."

Jesus Turns Water Into Wine
JN 2:1-12

On the third day, Jesus, his disciples, and his mother Mary attended a wedding at Cana in Galilee.

When the wine ran out, Mary told Jesus, "All the wine is gone."

"Dear woman, why do you involve me?" he replied. "My hour has not yet come."

"Do whatever he tells you," Mary told the servants.

Six stone water jars were nearby that the Jews commonly used for ceremonial washing — each could hold from 20 to 30 gallons.

"Fill those jars with water," Jesus told the servants.

So they filled them to the brim.

"Now take some to the host of the banquet."

They took it to him and the host drank water that had been turned into wine. He didn't know where it had come from, but the servants who had filled the jars did.

He called the bridegroom and said, "Everyone serves the best wine first and the cheaper wine after the guests have had too much to drink, but you saved the best for last."

So Jesus performed his first miracle at Cana. In this way he revealed his glory and his disciples believed in him. Then Jesus went down to Capernaum for a few days with his mother, his brothers, and his disciples.

Jesus Clears the Temple
JN 2:13-25

When it was almost time for the Passover, Jesus went up to Jerusalem. He found men in the temple courts selling cattle, sheep, and doves. Others sat at tables exchanging money. So Jesus made a whip out of cords and drove them all from the temple area, both sheep and cattle; he scattered the moneychangers' coins and overturned their tables. To those who sold doves he said, "Get them out of here! How dare you turn my Father's house into a marketplace!"

And his disciples remembered that it is written, *Zeal for your house will consume me.*

The Jews asked him, "What miracle can you perform to demonstrate your authority to do this?"

"Destroy this temple and I will raise it again in three days," Jesus replied.

"It took 46 years to build this temple; how are you going to raise it in 3 days?"

They didn't realize the temple Jesus had spoken about was his body.

After he was raised from the dead, his disciples recalled that he had said this, and they believed in his words and in the Scripture.

Jesus performed miracles at the Passover Feast and many people believed in him. But he wouldn't entrust himself to them, because he understood human nature. He didn't need anyone to tell him about humans, because he knew what they were really like.

Jesus Teaches Nicodemus
JN 3:1-21

One day a Pharisee and leader who was a member of the Jewish ruling council visited Jesus at night. His name was Nicodemus.

"Rabbi," he said, "we know you're a teacher who came from God. No one could perform such miracles if God wasn't with him."

"I assure you," Jesus said, "no one can enter God's kingdom unless he is born again."

"How can a man be born when he is old?" Nicodemus asked. "Surely he can't enter again into his mother's womb!"

"I assure you, no one can enter God's kingdom unless he is born of water and of the Spirit. Flesh gives birth to flesh, but the Spirit gives birth to spirit. You shouldn't be surprised that I say you must be born again. The wind blows wherever it pleases. You hear its sound, but you can't tell where it comes from or where it's going. It's the same with everyone born of the Spirit."

"How is this possible?"

"You're Israel's teacher and you don't understand these things?" Jesus asked. "I assure you, we speak of what we know and testify about what we've seen, but you people still don't accept our testimony. I speak to you about earthly things and you don't believe — how will you believe if I speak about heavenly things? No one who has gone to heaven has ever returned. But I, the Son of Man, came down from heaven. Just as Moses lifted up the snake in the desert, so the Son of Man must be lifted up, so that everyone who believes in him can have eternal life.

"For God so loved the world that he gave his one and only Son, so that no one who believes in him will perish but have eternal life. God didn't send his Son into the world to condemn the world, but to save it through him. No one who believes in him is condemned, but whoever doesn't believe is already condemned, because he doesn't believe in the name of God's one and only Son. This is the verdict: Light came into the world, but men loved darkness instead of light because the things they did were evil. Those who do evil hate the light, and they won't enter into it, because they're afraid that their activities will be exposed. But whoever lives by the truth enters the light, allowing everyone to clearly see that what they have done was accomplished through God."

John Testifies About Jesus
JN 3:22-23|JN 3:25-36|JN 4:1-2

Jesus spent some time with his disciples, baptizing in the Judean countryside. John also baptized at Aenon near Salim. There was plenty of water there, and people constantly came to be baptized.

Now the Pharisees heard that Jesus was accumulating and baptizing more disciples than John, but it was his disciples who actually did the baptizing, not Jesus.

John's disciples and one of the Jews began arguing about ceremonial washing, so they went to John and said, "Rabbi, that man you testified about who was with you on the other side of the Jordan is baptizing people. Everyone is going to him!"

John replied, "A man can receive only what heaven gives him. Don't you remember I said I'm not the Christ but was sent to prepare the way for him? The groom marries the bride, but the groom's friend stands with him. He listens and is filled with joy when he hears the groom's voice. In the same way, my joy is now complete. He must become greater; I must become less.

"The one who comes from above is above all; the one who is from the earth belongs to the earth and speaks as one from the earth. The one who comes from heaven is above all. He testifies about what he saw and heard, but no one accepts his testimony. Whoever accepts his testimony confirms that God is truthful. The one whom God sent speaks the words of God, because God gives the Spirit generously. The Father loves the Son and has placed everything in his hands. Whoever believes in the Son has eternal life, but whoever rejects the Son will experience God's wrath of judgment."

Now Herod was the ruler of Galilee, and he had married Herodias, his brother Philip's wife. John had been reprimanding Herod for all the evil things he had done and telling him, "It's against the law to marry your brother's wife."

So Herod added to his many crimes and ordered that John be tied up and put in prison. After John was arrested, Jesus left Judea and traveled back to Galilee.

On his way to Galilee, Jesus was compelled to travel through Samaria. He arrived in the city of Sychar, which was near the land Jacob had given to his son Joseph.

Jesus was tired from the journey, so he sat down by Jacob's well while his disciples went into the city to buy food. At about noon a Samaritan woman came to draw water.

"Can I have a drink?" Jesus asked.

"You're a Jew and I'm a Samaritan woman," she said. "How can you ask me for a drink?" (Jews don't associate with Samaritans.)

"If you knew the gift of God and who is asking you for a drink, you would ask and I would give you living water."

"Sir," the woman said, "the well is deep and you don't have a bucket. Where will you get this living water? Are you greater than our father Jacob who gave us this well? He drank from it, along with his sons and livestock."

Jesus answered, "Everyone who drinks this water will be thirsty again, but whoever drinks the water I give will never thirst. In fact, it will become a spring welling up inside to eternal life."

"Sir, give me this water so I won't get thirsty and have to keep coming to this well for water."

"Go get your husband and come back."

"I don't have a husband," she replied.

"You've told the truth," Jesus said. "You've had five husbands, and the man you're with now isn't your husband."

"Sir," the woman said, "you're obviously a prophet. Our fathers worshiped on this mountain, but you Jews say we must worship in Jerusalem."

"Dear woman, believe me — a time is coming when you will worship the Father neither on this mountain nor in Jerusalem. You Samaritans don't understand who you worship, but we know who we worship because salvation comes from the Jews. Yet a time is coming, and is now here, when true worshipers will worship the Father in spirit and truth. These are the kind of worshipers the Father seeks. God is spirit, and his worshipers must worship in spirit and in truth."

"I know that the Messiah is coming," the woman said. "He will explain everything to us."

"I Am He," Jesus said.

The Fields Are Ripe for Harvest
JN 4:27-38

Jesus' disciples returned and were surprised to find him talking to a woman. But no one asked, "What do you want?" or "Why are you talking to her?"

Then the woman left her water jar and went back to the city. "Come see a man who told me everything I ever did," she told the people. "Could he be the Messiah?"

So they left the city and went to go see him.

In the meantime, his disciples urged him, "Rabbi, have something to eat."

"I have food to eat that you know nothing about," Jesus said.

"Did someone bring him food?" they asked each other.

"My food is to do the will of him who sent me and to finish his work. You have a saying: 'Four months more and then comes the harvest.' So open your eyes and see that the fields are ripe for harvest. The reaper is already receiving his wages and harvesting the crop for eternal life, so that the sower and the reaper will rejoice together. So the saying 'One sows and another reaps' is true. I sent you to reap what you didn't work for. Others did the hard work and you reaped the benefits of their labor."

Samaritans Believe in Jesus
JN 4:39-43

Many Samaritans believed in Jesus because the woman had testified, "He told me everything I ever did." They urged him to stay with them, so he stayed two days. And many more became believers because of his teaching.

They said to the woman, "Now we believe not just because of what you told us but because we've heard him for ourselves. He really is the Savior of the world!"

After the two days, Jesus left for Galilee.

PART II
JESUS' GALILEAN
MINISTRY

CHAPTER 3
Teachings and Healings in Galilee & Jerusalem

Jesus Begins Teaching in Galilee
MT 4:17|MK 1:14b-15|LK 4:14-15|JN 4:45

Jesus returned to Galilee in the power of the Spirit, and the Galileans welcomed him because they saw everything he had done in Jerusalem at the Passover Feast.

From that time on, Jesus began to preach, "The time has come and the kingdom of heaven is near. Repent and believe the good news!"

And news about him spread throughout the whole countryside. He taught in their synagogues and everyone praised him.

Jesus Heals the Official's Son
JN 4:46-54

Jesus visited Cana in Galilee again, where he had turned water into wine. A royal official heard that Jesus had arrived and he went and begged him to heal his son, who was sick at Capernaum and close to death.

"You people will never believe unless you see miracles and wonders," Jesus said.

"Sir, come down before my child dies," the official said.

"Go," Jesus replied, "your son will live."

The man believed Jesus and headed home. While he was still on the way, his servants met him and told him his son was alive and well. He asked when he had gotten better and they said, "The fever left him yesterday at 1pm."

He realized this was the exact moment at which Jesus had said his son would live, so he and his household believed.

This was the second miracle Jesus performed after coming from Judea to Galilee.

The People Reject Jesus at Nazareth
MT 4:13-16|MT 13:53-58|MK 6:1-6a|LK 4:16-30|JN 4:44

Accompanied by his disciples, Jesus went to Nazareth, where he had grown up. He went to the synagogue on the Sabbath, as was his habit, and someone gave him the scroll of the prophet Isaiah. He unrolled it, found his place, and stood up to read: *"The Spirit of the Lord is upon me. He has anointed me to preach good news to the poor, to proclaim freedom for the prisoners and recover sight for the blind, to release the oppressed, and to proclaim the year of the Lord's favor."*

He rolled up the scroll, gave it back to the attendant, and sat down. As everyone stared at him, he said, "Today, this scripture has been fulfilled."

They all complimented him, amazed at his gracious words. "Where did he get such wisdom and miraculous powers?" they asked. "Isn't he the son of Joseph the carpenter? Isn't his mother Mary, and his brothers James, Joseph, Simon, and Judas? Don't all his sisters live among us? Where did he learn all these things?"

Jesus said, "I know you want to quote this proverb to me: 'Physician, heal yourself! Do the same miracles in your hometown that you did in Capernaum.' I assure you, a prophet is without honor only in his hometown, among his relatives, and in his own household. There were many widows in Israel in Elijah's time, when the sky was shut for three and a half years and there was a severe famine throughout the land. Yet Elijah was sent only to a widow in Zarephath, in the region of Sidon. And many people in Israel had leprosy during the time of Elisha the prophet, but only Naaman the Syrian was cleansed."

The people in the synagogue were furious and offended, so they ran him out of the city and took him to the edge of the hill on which the city was built. They intended to throw him over the cliff, but he walked right through the crowd and went on his way.

Jesus didn't do many miracles there, except heal a few sick people. And he was amazed at their lack of faith. He left Nazareth and went to live in Capernaum, which was by the lake in the area of Zebulun and Naphtali. This fulfilled the words of the prophet Isaiah: *Land of Zebulun and land of Naphtali — along the sea and beyond the Jordan — Galilee of the Gentiles. The people living in darkness have seen the great light that has dawned on those living in the shadowland of death.*

Jesus Calls Four Fishermen
MT 4:18-22|MK 1:16-20|LK 5:1-11

One day Jesus was teaching God's word by the Sea of Galilee (also known as Lake Gennesaret), and the crowd was pressing in on him. Two boats sat near the water's edge that had been left there by the fishermen, and Peter and his brother Andrew were washing their nets in the sea. Jesus got into Peter's boat and asked him to row out a little from the shore. He then sat down and taught the people.

When he finished he said, "Peter, row out into deep water and let down the nets for a catch."

"Master, we worked hard all night and didn't catch anything," Peter replied, "but because you say so, we will let down the nets."

They did so and caught such a large number of fish that their nets began to break. So they signaled their partners — James and his brother John — who were in a boat with their father Zebedee, preparing their nets. They filled both boats to the point that they began to sink. And Peter and his friends were amazed at such a great catch of fish.

Then Peter fell at Jesus' feet and said, "Leave me, Lord; I'm a sinful man!"

"Don't be afraid," Jesus said. "Follow me and I will make you fishers of men."

So Peter and Andrew pulled their boats up to the shore, left everything, and followed him.

Jesus also called James and John; they left their father in the boat with the hired men and followed him also.

Jesus Drives Out a Demon
MK 1:21-28|LK 4:31-37

They went to Capernaum in Galilee, and Jesus taught in the synagogue on the Sabbath. Everyone was amazed because he taught as someone who had authority and not as the teachers of the law.

At that moment a man possessed by a demon shouted, "What do you want with us, Jesus of Nazareth? Did you come to destroy us? I know who you are — the Holy One of God!"

"Be quiet and come out of him," Jesus said firmly.

The demon sent the man into convulsions, threw him down, and came out screaming. But the man wasn't injured.

The people were amazed and said to each other, "He commands demons with power and authority, and they come out! Is this some kind of new teaching?"

So news about Jesus spread quickly throughout the whole region of Galilee.

Jesus Heals Peter's Mother-in-Law and Others
MT 8:14-17|MK 1:29-34|LK 4:38-41

They left the synagogue and took James and John and went to Peter and Andrew's house. Peter's mother-in-law was in bed with a high fever, so they asked Jesus to heal her.

Jesus leaned over her and rebuked the fever, and the fever left. Then he took her hand and helped her up, and she began to serve them.

That evening after sunset, the people brought the sick and demon-possessed to Jesus. He drove out many demons with a word and they came out shouting, "You are the Son of God!" But Jesus rebuked them and stopped them from speaking, because they knew he was the Christ. The whole city had gathered at the door, and Jesus laid his hands on each one and healed them of various diseases. This fulfilled the words spoken through the prophet Isaiah: *He took up our weaknesses and carried our diseases.*

Jesus Prays in a Secluded Place
MK 1:35-38|LK 4:42-43

Very early in the morning while it was still dark, Jesus left the house and went to a secluded place to pray.

The people were searching for him, so Peter and the other disciples found Jesus and said, "Everyone is looking for you."

When the people eventually found him, they tried to prevent him from leaving.

Then Jesus said to his disciples, "I must preach the good news of God's kingdom to the other cities also, so let's go to the nearby villages, because that's why I was sent."

Jesus Preaches and Heals in Galilee
MT 4:23-25|MK 1:39|LK 4:44

Jesus went throughout Galilee teaching in synagogues, preaching the good news of the kingdom, and healing every sickness and disease. News about him spread throughout Syria, and people brought him those who were sick with various diseases, suffering severe pain, having seizures, demon-possessed, and paralyzed. And Jesus healed them all. Large crowds followed him from Galilee, the Decapolis, Jerusalem, Judea, and the region across the Jordan.

Jesus Heals a Man's Leprosy
MT 8:1-4|MK 1:40-45|LK 5:12-16

While Jesus was in one of the cities, a man covered with leprosy saw him. He fell on his knees and bowed with his face to the ground. "Lord," he begged, "if you're willing, you can make me clean."

Jesus was filled with compassion and he touched the man. "I'm willing," he said. "Be cleansed!"

He was cured immediately and Jesus sent him away, warning, "Don't tell anyone about this but go show yourself to the priest. As a testimony, offer the sacrifices that Moses commanded for your cleansing."

But the man left and talked freely about his healing. So the news about Jesus kept spreading and crowds came to hear him and be healed. As a result, Jesus couldn't enter a city openly but often withdrew to secluded places to pray.

But the people still came to him from everywhere.

Jesus Heals a Paralytic
MT 9:2-8|MK 2:1-12|LK 5:17-26

A few days later, Jesus went to Capernaum again and the people heard that he had returned home. So many people had gathered that there was no room left, not even outside the door, and he preached the word to them.

The Pharisees and teachers of the law were also sitting there, having come from all the villages of Galilee, Judea, and Jerusalem.

Now the power of the Lord was present for him to heal the sick. Four men arrived carrying a paralytic. They tried to take him into the house to lay him before Jesus, but they couldn't because of the crowd. So they dug through the tiles on the roof and made a hole right above Jesus. Then they lowered the paralyzed man on his mat into the middle of the crowd, right in front of Jesus.

Jesus was impressed with their faith and said to the paralytic, "Son, be encouraged; your sins are forgiven."

The Pharisees and the teachers of the law thought to themselves, *Who is this man who speaks blasphemy? No one can forgive sins but God alone.*

Jesus knew immediately what they were thinking. "Why do you entertain evil thoughts?" he asked. "Is it easier to say 'Your sins are forgiven' or to say 'Get up and walk'? But now you will know that the Son of Man has authority on earth to forgive sins."

So he said to the paralytic, "Get up, take your mat, and go home."

Immediately the man got up in front of everyone and went home praising God.

They were amazed and praised God for giving such authority. "We've never seen anything like this!" they said.

Jesus Calls Matthew
MT 9:9-13|MK 2:13|MK 2:14b|MK 2:15-17|LK 5:27-32

One day Jesus went to the lake and taught the large crowd that had assembled there. Later as he was walking along, he saw Matthew sitting at the tax collector's booth.

"Follow me," Jesus said.

Matthew left everything and followed him. Then he held a great banquet for Jesus at his house and because many tax collectors and sinners followed Jesus, they ate with him and his disciples.

The teachers of the law and the Pharisees asked his disciples, "Why is he eating with tax collectors and sinners?"

Jesus heard them and replied, "It's not the healthy who need a doctor, but the sick. Now go and learn what this means, *I desire mercy, not sacrifice.* I didn't come to call the righteous to repentance, but sinners."

John's Disciples Question Jesus About Fasting
MT 9:14-17|MK 2:18-22|LK 5:33-39

Now John's disciples and the Pharisees were fasting, so John's disciples said to Jesus, "The Pharisees' disciples fast and pray often, and so do we. Why do yours continue eating and drinking?"

"The bridegroom's guests don't mourn while he's with them," Jesus said. "But when the bridegroom is finally taken from them, then they will fast."

And he told them this parable:

> No one tears a patch from a new garment and sews it onto an old one. He would tear the new garment, and the patch from the new wouldn't match the old. Instead, it would pull away from the garment, making the tear worse. In the same way, no one pours new wine into old wineskins. The new wine would burst the skins, the wine would run out, and the wineskins would be ruined. New wine must be poured into new wineskins so that both are preserved. But no one wants the new after drinking the old, because he thinks the old wine is better.

Jesus Heals a Man at Bethesda Pool
JN 5:1-15

Some time later Jesus went up to Jerusalem for a Jewish feast. There was a pool near the Sheep Gate, which in Aramaic is called *Bethesda*. It was surrounded by five covered areas where many disabled people lay — the blind, the crippled, and the paralyzed.

Jesus saw a man lying there who had been an invalid for 38 years, so he asked him, "Do you want to get well?"

"Sir," the man replied, "there's no one to help me get into the pool when the water is stirred. Someone always gets in before me."

"Get up!" Jesus said. "Pick up your mat and walk."

Immediately the man was healed, so he picked up his mat and walked.

Then the Jews said to him, "Today is the Sabbath, and the law forbids you to carry your mat."

"But the man who healed me told me to," he said.

"Who is this man?"

Since Jesus had disappeared into the crowd, he couldn't tell them who it was.

Later Jesus found him at the temple and said, "Now that you're well again, stop sinning or something worse might happen to you."

So the man told the Jews that it was Jesus who had healed him.

Jesus Teaches About His Authority
JN 5:16-47

Then the Jews criticized Jesus because he had healed on the Sabbath.

So Jesus said, "My Father is always working, even now, and I'm working too."

This made the Jews more determined to kill him. Not only was he breaking the Sabbath, he was calling God his own Father, making himself equal with God.

"I assure you," Jesus said. "The Son can't do anything by himself; he can do only what he sees his Father doing. He does whatever the Father does because the Father loves the Son and shows him everything he's doing. He will show him even greater things than these, and all of you will be amazed. Just as the Father raises the dead and gives them life, the Son also gives life to whomever he pleases. Likewise, the Father doesn't judge anyone but has entrusted all judgment to the Son. He did this so all people will honor the Son just as they honor the Father. Those who don't honor the Son don't honor the Father who sent him.

"I assure you, whoever listens to me and believes in the One who sent me has eternal life. He won't be condemned — he will cross over from death to life. A time is coming — in fact, it has already come — when those who are dead will hear the voice of the Son of God, and they will live. Just as the Father has life in himself, he has also granted the Son to have life in himself. And he gave him the authority to judge because he is the Son of Man.

"Don't be surprised. A time is coming when those in their graves will hear his voice and come out — those who did good will rise and live, and those who did evil will rise and be condemned. I can't do anything on my own authority, I judge only as instructed, and my judgment is fair because I'm not trying to please myself but the One who sent me.

"If I testify on my own behalf, my testimony isn't valid. But there's someone else who testifies for me and his testimony is valid. You sent messengers to John and he testified to the truth. This doesn't mean I need a human witness, but I'm bringing it up so you will be saved. John was a burning and shining lamp, and you chose for a little while to enjoy his light.

"But I have a witness greater than John. The work that the Father gave me to finish testifies that he sent me. In fact, the Father himself testified about me. You've never seen him or heard his voice, and his word doesn't live within you, because you don't believe the one he sent. You carefully study the Scriptures because you think they've given you eternal life. These same Scriptures testify about me, yet you refuse to allow me to give you life.

"I don't need praise from men, but I know you and you don't have the love of God in your hearts. I came in my Father's name, but you don't accept me. However, you accept anyone else who comes in his own name. How will you believe if you accept praise from one another but make no effort to gain the praise that comes from the one and only God?

"But I won't be the one to accuse you before the Father. Moses, in whom you've placed your hope, is the one who will accuse you. If you really believed Moses, you would believe me, because he wrote about me. But since you don't believe what he wrote, how will you believe what I say?"

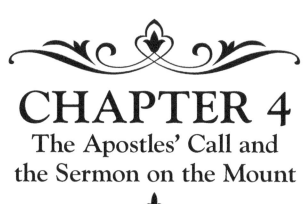

CHAPTER 4
The Apostles' Call and
the Sermon on the Mount

Jesus Demonstrates Lordship Over the Sabbath
MT 12:1-14|MK 2:23-28|MK 3:1-6|LK 6:1-11

One Sabbath Jesus was walking through the grain fields. His disciples were hungry, so they picked some heads of grain, rubbed them in their hands, and ate the kernels.

"Look," the Pharisees said to Jesus, "your disciples are breaking the Sabbath law!"

"Haven't you read the scriptures?" Jesus asked. "When Abiathar was high priest, David and his companions were hungry. So David entered the house of God and ate the sacred bread, which is lawful only for priests to eat. He even gave some to his companions.

"Furthermore, haven't you read in the Law that the priests in the temple violate the Sabbath and yet are innocent? But one greater than the temple is here. If you understood these words, *I desire mercy, not sacrifice,* you wouldn't condemn the innocent. The Sabbath was made for man, not man for the Sabbath. Therefore the Son of Man is Lord even over the Sabbath."

On another Sabbath Jesus went to the synagogue to teach, and a man was there whose right hand was paralyzed. The Pharisees and the teachers of the law wanted a reason to bring charges against Jesus, so they watched him closely to see if he would heal on the Sabbath.

Jesus knew what they were thinking, so he said to the man with the paralyzed hand, "Stand up."

And the man did.

The Jewish leaders asked him, "Is it lawful to heal on the Sabbath?"

Jesus replied, "Is it lawful on the Sabbath to do good or to do evil, to save a life or to kill? If your sheep falls into a pit on the Sabbath, wouldn't you lift it out? Isn't a man more valuable than a sheep?"

They all remained silent.

Jesus looked at them in anger, deeply distressed because of their stubborn hearts. Then he said to the man, "Stretch out your hand."

When he did, his hand was completely healed, just as good as the other.

The Pharisees were furious, so they left and began planning with the Herodians how to kill Jesus.

Jesus Teaches by the Sea
MT 12:15-21|MK 3:7-12|LK 6:17-19

Jesus was aware that they were planning to kill him, so he withdrew with his disciples to the sea. But a large crowd from Galilee followed him there. Others who heard about everything he was doing followed him from Judea, Jerusalem, Idumea, the regions across the Jordan, and around Tyre and Sidon. They came to hear him teach and to be healed of their diseases. Everyone tried to touch him because power was coming from him and healing them all.

Those troubled by demons were delivered. The demons saw Jesus and fell down before him, crying out, "You are the Son of God!" But he sternly ordered them not to reveal who he was.

This fulfilled the words spoken through the prophet Isaiah: *This is my chosen servant, the one I love, in whom I delight. I will put my Spirit upon him and he will proclaim justice to the nations. He won't argue or shout, and no one will hear his voice in the streets. He won't break a bruised reed or extinguish a smoldering wick until he leads justice to victory, and the nations will put their hope in his name.*

Jesus told his disciples to prepare a small boat to keep the people from crowding him.

Jesus Chooses 12 Apostles
MT 5:1|MT 10:1-4|MK 2:14a|MK 3:13-19
LK 6:12-16|JN 1:45a|JN 11:16a

Later Jesus ascended the mountain and spent the night praying to God. In the morning he assembled his disciples and chose 12 of them to be apostles. They would travel with him so he could send them out to preach and give them authority to drive out demons.

These are the names of the 12 apostles:

[1] **Simon**, to whom Jesus gave the name Peter

[2] **Andrew**, Peter's brother

[3] **James** and his brother, [4] **John** (Zebedee's sons) — Jesus gave them the name *Boanerges*, which means *Sons of Thunder*
[5] **Philip**
[6] **Bartholomew** — also known as Nathanael
[7] **Thomas** — also known as Didymus
[8] **Matthew**, the tax collector (son of Alphaeus) — also known as Levi
[9] **James** (son of Alphaeus)
[10] **Thaddaeus** (son of James) — also known as Judas
[11] **Simon the Zealot**
[12] **Judas Iscariot**, who betrayed Jesus

The Sermon on the Mount

The Beatitudes
MT 5:1-12|LK 6:20-26

Then Jesus sat down and taught them, saying:
"Blessed are the poor in spirit, for theirs is the kingdom of heaven.
Blessed are those who mourn, for they will be comforted.
Blessed are the gentle, for they will inherit the earth.
Blessed are those who hunger and thirst for righteousness, for they will be satisfied.
Blessed are those who weep, for they will laugh.
Blessed are the merciful, for they will be shown mercy.
Blessed are the pure in heart, for they will see God.
Blessed are the peacemakers, for they will be called children of God.
Blessed are those who are persecuted because of righteousness, for theirs is the kingdom of heaven.
"Blessed are you when others hate you, exclude you, insult you, persecute you, and falsely speak every kind of evil against you because of me. Rejoice and be glad, because your reward in heaven will be great. This is the same way their ancestors treated the prophets before you.
"But woe to you who are rich, for you've already received your comfort.
Woe to you who are well-fed now, for you will go hungry.
Woe to you who laugh now, for you will mourn and weep.
Woe to you when everyone speaks well of you, for their ancestors also spoke well of the false prophets."

Be the Salt of the Earth
MT 5:13|MK 9:50|LK 14:34-35

"You are the salt of the earth. Salt is good but if it loses its saltiness, how can it be made salty again? It's fit neither for the soil nor for the manure pile; it is thrown out and trampled by men. Those who have ears to hear, let them hear. Have salt in yourselves and be at peace with each other."

Be Light to the World
MT 5:14-16|MT 6:22-23|MK 4:21-23
LK 8:16-17|LK 11:33-36

"You are the light of the world. A city built on a hill cannot be hidden. Do you light a lamp and put it under a bowl or under a bed? No, you put it on a stand so it can provide light to everyone in the house. Whatever is hidden is meant to be exposed, and whatever is concealed is meant to be revealed. Those who have ears to hear, let them hear.

"Your eye is the lamp of your body. When your eyes are healthy, your whole body also is full of light. But when they are unhealthy, your body is full of darkness. Make sure what's within you is not darkness, for if it is, how great that darkness will be! When your whole body is full of light — with no sign of darkness — it will be completely illuminated, just as if a lamp shined its light on you. In the same way, let your light shine before others so they can see your good deeds and praise your Father in heaven."

Jesus Fulfills the Law
MT 5:17-20|LK 16:17

"Don't assume that I came to abolish the Law or the Prophets; I didn't come to abolish them but to fulfill them. I assure you, until heaven and earth disappear, neither the smallest letter nor the smallest stroke of a pen will disappear from the Law until everything is accomplished. Anyone who breaks even the least of these commandments and teaches others to do the same will be called least in the kingdom of heaven, but whoever practices and teaches these commands will be called great in the kingdom of heaven. I assure you, unless your righteousness exceeds that of the Pharisees and the teachers of the law, you most certainly won't enter the kingdom of heaven."

Don't Commit Murder
MT 5:21-26

"You have heard that it was said long ago, 'Don't commit murder; anyone who does is subject to judgment.' But I'm telling you that anyone who is angry with his brother is subject to judgment. And anyone who says to his brother, 'You idiot' must answer to the Sanhedrin." (Idiot is *Raca* in Aramaic.) "But anyone who says, 'You wicked scoundrel!' is in danger of hell's fire. So if you're offering your gift at the altar and remember that your brother is angry with you, leave your gift there. First go and reconcile with your brother and then return and offer your gift.

"Reach a settlement quickly with your adversary while you are on the way to court. Otherwise he will turn you over to the judge, who will turn you over to the officer to be thrown into prison. You most certainly won't get out until you pay every penny."

Don't Commit Adultery
MT 5:27-30|MT 18:8-9|MK 9:43-49

"You have heard it said, 'Don't commit adultery.' But I'm telling you that anyone who looks at a woman lustfully has already committed adultery with her in his heart. If your right hand or foot causes you to sin, cut it off and throw it away. It's better for you to enter the kingdom of God disfigured or crippled than to have two hands or two feet and be thrown into eternal fire. It's better to lose one part of your body than for your whole body to be thrown into hell. And if your right eye causes you to sin, gouge it out and throw it away. It's better for you to enter the kingdom of God with one eye than to have two eyes and be thrown into the fire of hell — where *the worms that feed on them never die and the fire is never quenched.* Everyone will be salted with fire."

Honor Your Promises
MT 5:33-37

"Again, you have heard that it was said long ago, 'Don't break your promise; keep the promises you've made to the Lord.' But I'm telling you not to swear at all: neither by heaven, for it's God's throne; nor by the earth, for it's his footstool; nor by Jerusalem, for it's the city of the Great King. Nor should you swear by your head, because you can't make even one hair white or black. Simply say 'Yes' or 'No'; anything beyond this comes from the evil one."

Love Your Enemies
MT 5:38-48|MT 7:12|LK 6:27-36

"You have heard that it was said, 'An eye for an eye and a tooth for a tooth.' But I'm telling you not to resist an evil person. If someone hits you on the right cheek, turn to him the other also. And if someone wants to sue you and take your shirt, let him have your coat as well. If someone forces you to go one mile, go with him two miles. Give to those who ask you and don't refuse those who want to borrow from you. If anyone takes what belongs to you, don't demand it back. In all things, do for others whatever you want them to do for you, because this sums up the Law and the Prophets.

"You have heard that it was said, 'Love your neighbor and hate your enemy.' But I'm telling all of you who are listening to love your enemies, do good to those who hate you, bless those who curse you, and pray for those who mistreat you. If you love those who love you, what credit is that to you? Even sinners and tax collectors love those who love them. And if you are good to those who are good to you, what credit is that to you? Even sinners and Gentiles do that. And if you lend to those from whom you expect repayment, what credit is that to you? Even sinners lend to sinners, expecting to be repaid in full. And if you greet only your brothers, what are you doing more than others? Don't even pagans do that?

"So love your enemies — treat them well and lend to them without expecting anything in return. Then your reward will be great and you will be children of your Father in heaven. He causes his sun to rise on the evil and the good and sends rain on the righteous and the unrighteous. Be merciful just as your Father is merciful. Be perfect, as your heavenly Father is perfect."

Don't Give or Fast for Show
MT 6:1-4|MT 6:16-18

"Be sure not to perform righteous acts just to show off for others. Your Father in heaven won't reward you for that. And don't announce it with trumpets when you give to the needy. The hypocrites do this in the synagogues and in the streets to be honored by others, but I assure you, they have received their reward in full. When you give to the needy, don't let your left hand know what your right hand is doing. Then your giving will be done in secret.

"And when you fast, don't look miserable like the hypocrites do. They purposely look gloomy to show others they are fasting. I assure you, they have received their reward in full. Instead, put oil on your head and wash your face. Then your fasting won't be obvious to others but only to your Father, who is unseen. And your Father, who sees what is done in secret, will reward you."

Store Your Treasures in Heaven
MT 6:19-21|MT 6:24|LK 12:32-34

"Don't be afraid, little flock — your Father is pleased to give you the kingdom. Sell your possessions and give to the poor. Don't store up for yourselves treasures on earth, where moth and rust destroy and thieves break in and steal. Instead, provide purses for yourselves that won't wear out. Store up inexhaustible treasures in heaven — where moth and rust don't destroy and thieves don't break in and steal. For where your treasure is, there your heart will be also.

"No one can serve two masters. Either you will hate the one and love the other, or you will be devoted to the one and despise the other. You cannot serve both God and money."

Don't Worry
MT 6:25-34|LK 12:22-31

"Don't worry about your life — what you will eat or drink — or about your body — what you will wear. Isn't life more than food and the body more than clothes? Consider the ravens. They don't plant or harvest; they have no storeroom or barn, yet your heavenly father feeds them. And you are much more valuable than birds!

"Why do you worry about clothes? Observe how the lilies of the field grow. They don't labor or sew clothes, but I assure you that not even Solomon in all his splendor was dressed like one of these. If that's how God clothes the grass, which is in the field today and thrown into the furnace tomorrow, isn't he more likely to clothe you? But you have so little faith!

"Can any of you add a single hour to your life by worrying? Since you can't do such a little thing, why worry about the rest? So don't worry about what you will eat, what you will drink, or what you will wear. Unbelievers are concerned about all these things, and your heavenly Father knows that you need them. But seek first his kingdom and his righteousness, and all these things will be given to you as well. Don't worry about to-morrow, because tomorrow will worry about itself. Each day has enough trouble of its own."

Judge Without Hypocrisy
MT 7:1-6|MK 4:24|LK 6:37-38|LK 6:41-42

"Don't judge and you won't be judged. Don't condemn and you won't be condemned. You will be judged in the same way you judge others. So why are you concerned about the speck of sawdust in your brother's eye but pay no attention to the log in your own eye? How can you say, 'Brother, let me take the speck out of your eye' when you fail to see the log in your own eye? You hypocrite! First take the log out of your own eye and then you will see clearly to remove the speck from your brother's eye.

"Forgive and you will be forgiven. Give and it will be given to you. A good measure — pressed down, shaken together, and running over — will be poured into your lap. The standard of measure you use for others is the same standard God will use for you.

"Don't give dogs what is sacred; don't throw your pearls to pigs. They may trample them under their feet and then tear you to pieces!"

Judge a Tree by Its Fruit
MT 7:15-20|LK 6:43-45

"Watch out for false prophets. They come to you in sheep's clothing, but inside they're ferocious wolves. You will recognize them by their fruit. Are grapes picked from thornbushes or figs from thistles? Every good tree produces good fruit, but a bad tree produces bad fruit. A good tree can't produce bad fruit and a bad tree can't produce good fruit. Every tree that doesn't produce good fruit is cut down and thrown into the fire.

"A good person produces good things out of the treasury of good in his heart, and an evil person produces evil things out of the treasury of evil in his heart — he speaks from the overflow of his heart. So you will recognize them by their fruit."

Enter the Narrow Gate
MT 7:13-14|MT 7:21-23|MT 8:11-12|LK 13:23-30

Someone asked Jesus, "Lord, will only a few people be saved?"

"Make every effort to enter through the narrow gate," he replied. "I assure you, many will try to enter and won't be able to. For wide is the gate and broad is the road that leads to destruction, and many enter through it. But small is the gate and narrow is the road that leads to life, and only a few find it.

"Not everyone who says to me, 'Lord, Lord,' will enter the kingdom of heaven, but only the person who does the will of my Father in heaven. Once the owner of the house gets up and closes the door, you will stand outside knocking and pleading, 'Sir, open the door for us.'

"But he will answer, 'I don't know you or where you come from.'

"Then you will say, 'Lord, Lord, didn't we prophesy, drive out demons, and perform many miracles in your name? We ate and drank with you and you taught in our streets.'

"And I will tell them plainly, 'I never knew you. Get away from me, you evildoers!'

"People will come from east and west and north and south to take their places at the feast with Abraham, Isaac, and Jacob in the kingdom of heaven. When you see them and all the prophets there but you yourselves, the subjects of the kingdom, thrown outside into the darkness, there will be weeping and gnashing of teeth. Indeed, those who are last will be first, and those who are first will be last."

The Wise and Foolish Builders
MT 7:24-29|LK 6:46-49

"Why do you call me, 'Lord, Lord,' and don't do what I say? Everyone who comes to me, hears my words, and acts on them is like a wise man building a house. He dug down deep and laid the foundation on rock. The rain brought a flood, the rivers rose and crashed against the house, and the winds blew and pounded against it, but the house didn't collapse, because its foundation was built on rock.

"But everyone who hears my words and doesn't act on them is like a foolish man who built his house on sand, which has no foundation. The rain brought a flood, the rivers rose and crashed against the house, and the winds blew and pounded against it. Immediately it collapsed with a huge crash and its destruction was complete."

The crowds were amazed at Jesus' teaching. Unlike their teachers of the law, he taught as one with authority.

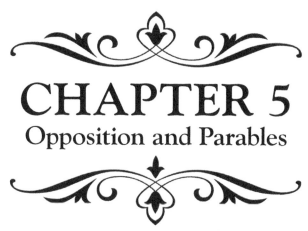

CHAPTER 5
Opposition and Parables

The Centurion Demonstrates Faith
MT 8:5-10|MT 8:13|LK 7:1-10

When Jesus finished teaching, he went to Capernaum and a centurion there heard about him. His servant whom he valued highly was sick and near death, so he sent some Jewish elders to ask Jesus to come heal him.

When they arrived they pleaded earnestly with Jesus, "Lord, his servant lies home paralyzed and suffering terribly. He deserves to have you come because he loves our nation and built our synagogue."

"I'll heal him," Jesus said.

He went with them and wasn't far from the house when the centurion sent friends to meet him with a message: "Lord, don't trouble yourself. I don't deserve to have you come to my house; that's why I didn't even consider myself worthy to come to you. But say the word and my servant will be healed. I myself am a man under authority, with soldiers who report to me. I tell one 'Go' and he goes, and another one 'Come' and he comes. I tell my servant 'Do this' and he does it."

Jesus was amazed and he said to the crowd following him, "I assure you, I haven't found such great faith even in Israel!"

Then Jesus said to the men, "Go! It will be done just as he believed it would."

So the men returned to the house and found the servant healed.

Jesus Raises a Widow's Son
LK 7:11-17

Then Jesus went to Nain, along with his disciples and a large crowd. As he approached the city gate, a dead man was being carried out — a widow's only son — accompanied by a large crowd from the city.

The Lord's heart went out to her. "Don't cry," he said.

He touched the open coffin and those carrying it stopped walking. "Young man, get up!" Jesus said.

The dead man sat up and spoke, and Jesus returned him to his mother.

Everyone was filled with awe and praised God. "A great prophet is among us," they said. "God has come to help his people."

So this news about Jesus spread throughout Judea and the surrounding country.

John the Baptist Questions Jesus
MT 11:2-19|LK 7:18-35

While John the Baptist was in prison, his disciples told him about everything Jesus was doing. So John sent two of them to ask the Lord, "Are you the one who was to come or should we expect someone else?"

At that very moment, Jesus cured many who had diseases, sicknesses, and evil spirits, and he gave sight to many who were blind. So he replied to the messengers, "Go tell John what you've seen and heard: The blind receive sight, the lame walk, those who have leprosy are cured, the deaf hear, the dead are raised, and the good news is preached to the poor. Blessed is the man who doesn't lose faith in me."

After the messengers left, Jesus spoke to the crowd about John: "What did you go out to the desert to see? A reed swayed by the wind? No? A man dressed in fine clothes? No, because those who wear expensive clothes and indulge in luxury live in palaces. So what did you go out to see? A prophet? Yes, I assure you, and more than a prophet. He is the one about whom it is written: *I'll send my messenger ahead of you, who will prepare your way before you.*"

Everyone, including the tax collectors, had acknowledged that God's way was right and had been baptized by John. But the Pharisees and experts in the law had rejected God's plan for themselves and refused to be baptized by John.

Jesus continued, "I assure you, no one is greater than John the Baptist, but he who is least in the kingdom of heaven is greater than John. From the days of John until now, the kingdom of heaven has been forcefully advancing, and violent people are attacking it. The Prophets and the Law prophesied until John came. And if you're willing to accept it, he is the Elijah who was to come.

"To what can I compare the people of this generation? What are they like? They're like children sitting in the marketplace calling out to each other: 'We played the flute for you and you didn't dance; we sang a sad song and you didn't cry.'

"John the Baptist came neither eating bread nor drinking wine and you say, 'He has a demon.' The Son of Man came eating and drinking and you say, 'He's a glutton and a drunkard, a friend of tax collectors and sinners.' But wisdom is proved right by all her children."

Jesus Condemns Unrepentant Cities
MT 11:20-30|LK 10:13-16|LK 10:21-24

Then Jesus condemned the cities in which he had performed most of his miracles, because they didn't repent. "Woe to you, Chorazin and Bethsaida! If the miracles that were performed in you had been performed in Tyre and Sidon, they would have repented long ago in sackcloth and ashes. But I assure you, it will be more bearable for Tyre and Sidon on the day of judgment than for you. And you, Capernaum, will you be exalted to heaven? No, you will go down to hades. If the miracles that were performed in you had been performed in Sodom, it would have remained until now. But I assure you that it will be more bearable for Sodom on the day of judgment than for you."

Then, full of joy through the Holy Spirit, Jesus said, "I praise you, Father, Lord of heaven and earth, because you've hidden these things from the wise and learned and revealed them to little children. Yes, Father, for this was your good pleasure. All things have been entrusted to me by my Father. No one knows who the Son is except the Father, and no one knows who the Father is except the Son, and those to whom the Son chooses to reveal him."

Then he turned to his disciples and said, "Blessed are the eyes that see the things you see. I assure you, many prophets and kings wanted to see them, but they didn't. Many wanted to hear the things you hear, but they didn't hear them. Whoever listens to you listens to me. Whoever rejects you rejects me. And whoever rejects me rejects the one who sent me."

He continued, "Come to me all you who are weary and burdened, and I will give you rest. Take my yoke upon you and learn from me, for I am gentle and humble, and you will find rest for your souls. For my yoke is easy and my burden is light."

A Sinful Woman Anoints Jesus
LK 7:36-50

One day a Pharisee named Simon invited Jesus to dinner, and a woman in that city who lived a sinful life learned that Jesus was there. As Jesus reclined at the table, she brought in an alabaster jar of perfume and stood behind him weeping, wetting his feet with her tears. Then she used her hair to wipe his feet, kissed them, and poured perfume on them.

Simon thought, *If this man were a prophet, he would know what kind of woman is touching him — that she's a sinner.*

"I have something to tell you, Simon," Jesus said.

"Tell me, teacher."

"Two men owed money to a certain moneylender. One owed him 500 denarii and the other owed 50. Neither of them had the money to pay him back, so he canceled both their debts. Now which of them will love him more?"

Simon replied, "I suppose the one who had the bigger debt canceled."

"You are correct. Take note of her, Simon," Jesus said, turning to the woman. "I came into your house and you gave me no water for my feet, but she wet my feet with her tears and wiped them with her hair. You didn't give me a kiss, but this woman hasn't stopped kissing my feet since I've been here. You didn't put oil on my head, but she poured perfume on my feet. Therefore I assure you, her many sins have been forgiven — because she loved much. But he who has been forgiven little loves little."

Jesus then said to the woman, "Your faith has saved you and your sins are forgiven. Go in peace."

The other guests said among themselves, "Who is this who even forgives sins?"

Women Follow Jesus
MK 16:9b|LK 8:1-3

Then Jesus traveled from one city and village to another, proclaiming the good news of the kingdom of God. The Twelve were with him, along with some women he had cured of evil spirits and diseases — one of them was Mary Magdalene, out of whom he had driven seven demons. The other women included Joanna the wife of Cuza — who was the manager of Herod's household; Susanna; and many more. These women helped support Jesus and the disciples with their own funds.

Jesus Heals the Blind and Mute
MT 9:27-31

Two blind men followed Jesus as he traveled, calling out, "Have mercy on us, Son of David!"

Then they approached Jesus when he went indoors and he asked them, "Do you believe I can heal you?"

"Yes, Lord," they replied.

Then he touched their eyes and said, "You will be healed because of your faith."

And their sight was restored.

"Don't tell anyone about this," Jesus sternly warned them.

But they spread the news about him all over that region.

Jesus Is Accused of Alliance With Beelzebub
MT 9:32-34|MT 12:22-37|MT 12:43-45|MK 3:22-30
LK 11:14-15|LK 11:17-26|LK 12:10

While they were leaving, someone brought Jesus a blind and mute man who was demon-possessed. After Jesus drove the demon out, the man could both talk and see.

Everyone was amazed and said, "Could this be the Son of David? Nothing like this has ever happened in Israel."

But the Pharisees said, "He's possessed by Beelzebub, the prince of demons. That's how he drives out demons."

Jesus knew what they were thinking, so he summoned them and said, "You claim that I drive out demons by Beelzebub, but how can Satan drive out Satan? He'd be divided against himself, so how could his kingdom stand? It couldn't, because his kingdom would end. A kingdom divided against itself cannot stand. A house divided against itself cannot stand.

"If I drive out demons by Beelzebub, by whom do your people drive them out? They will be your judges. But if I drive out demons by the Spirit of God, then the kingdom of God has come upon you.

"When a fully armed strong man guards his own house, his possessions are safe. But if someone stronger attacks him, overpowers him, and ties him up, he can take away the armor in which the man trusted. Only then can he rob his house and steal his possessions. He who isn't with me is against me, and he who doesn't gather with me scatters.

"When an evil spirit comes out of a man, it goes through waterless places seeking rest but doesn't find it. Then it says, 'I'll return to the house I left.' It arrives and finds the house unoccupied, swept, and put in order. Then it gathers seven other spirits more wicked than itself and they all go live there. So the final condition of that man is worse than the first. That's how it will be with this wicked generation.

"A good tree will produce good fruit and a bad tree will produce bad fruit, for a tree is recognized by its fruit. You brood of vipers, since you are evil, how then can you say anything good? The mouth speaks whatever is stored in your heart. A good man brings forth good from the good stored within him, and an evil man brings forth evil from the evil stored within him.

Every sin and blasphemy will be forgiven. Anyone who speaks a word against the Son of Man will be forgiven, but anyone who speaks against the Holy Spirit will never be forgiven, neither in this age nor in the age to come — he is guilty of an eternal sin. I assure you, everyone will give account on the day of judgment for every careless word he has spoken.

For by your words you will be acquitted, and by your words you will be condemned."

He said all this because they said he was possessed by a demon.

The Jewish Leaders Demand a Sign
MT 12:38-42|LK 11:16|LK 11:27-32

As the crowds were increasing, some of the Pharisees and teachers of the law said, "Teacher, we want you to perform a miraculous sign."

"A wicked and adulterous generation asks for a miraculous sign," Jesus replied, "but none will be given it except the sign of the prophet Jonah. Just as he was three days and three nights in the belly of a huge fish, so the Son of Man will be three days and three nights in the heart of the earth. Just as Jonah was a sign to the Ninevites, so the Son of Man will be a sign to this generation.

"The men of Nineveh will stand up at the judgment with this generation and condemn it, for they repented when Jonah preached, and now one greater than Jonah is here. The Queen of the South will rise at the judgment with this generation and condemn it, because she came from the ends of the earth to listen to Solomon's wisdom and now one greater than Solomon is here."

A woman in the crowd called out, "Blessed is the mother who gave you life and nursed you."

Jesus replied, "Blessed rather are those who hear the word of God and obey it."

Jesus' Mother and Brothers Worry About Him
MT 12:46-50|MK 3:20-21|MK 3:31-35|LK 8:19-21

Jesus went home and a crowd gathered, not even giving them time to eat. Jesus' family heard about everything he was saying and doing, and they thought he was crazy. They went to force him to come home, but they couldn't get near him because of the crowd. So they stood outside and sent someone in to get him.

Jesus was still speaking when someone told him, "Your mother and brothers are outside waiting to speak to you."

"Who is my mother and who are my brothers?" Jesus asked. Pointing to his disciples, who sat in a circle around him, he said, "Here are my mother and my brothers. For whoever hears the will of my Father in heaven, and does it, is my brother and sister and mother."

The Parable of the Sower
MT 13:1-9|MT 13:18-23|MK 4:1-9
MK 4:13-20|LK 8:4-9|LK 8:11-15

That same day Jesus left the house and sat by the lake. A large crowd gathered as people flocked to him from every city. There were so many people that he got into a boat on the lake and sat down, while the people stayed along the shore at the water's edge. Then he taught in parables:

> A farmer went out to plant his seed. As he scattered it, some fell along the path. But it was trampled on and the birds of the air ate it.

> Some fell on rocky places, where there wasn't much soil. It sprang up quickly because the soil was shallow. But the sun came up and scorched the plants, and they withered because they had no root and lacked moisture.

> Other seed fell among thorns, which grew up with it and choked the plants, so they didn't bear grain. Other seed fell on good soil. It grew and produced a crop, multiplying 30, 60, or even 100 times.

"He who has ears to hear, let him hear," Jesus concluded.

His disciples asked him what the parable meant.

"If you don't understand this parable, how will you understand any parable?" Jesus asked. "The seed is the word of God. When anyone hears the message about the kingdom and doesn't understand it, the devil takes away the word from their hearts so they won't believe and be saved. This is the seed planted along the path.

"The one who received the seed that fell on rocky places is the person who hears the word and immediately receives it with joy. He believes for a while but when he is tested, when trouble or persecution comes because of the word, he quickly falls away because he has no root.

"Still others hear the word and receive it like seed planted among thorns. The worries of this world, the deceitfulness of wealth, and the desires for other things choke the word, and they don't mature.

"But the one who received the seed that fell on good soil is the man with a noble and good heart. He hears the word and accepts it, and by persevering, he produces a crop yielding 100, 60, or 30 times what was planted."

"What is the kingdom of God like?" Jesus asked. "What parables should we use to describe it? It's like this:

A man scatters seed on the ground. Night and day, whether he's asleep or awake, the seed sprouts and grows, though he doesn't know how. All by itself, the soil produces grain — first the stalk, then the head, then the full kernel in the head. He gets his sickle as soon as the grain is ripe, because the harvest has come."

The kingdom of heaven is like a mustard seed that a man planted in his field. Even though it's the smallest of all your seeds, it grows into the largest of garden plants. It becomes a tree with such big branches that the birds of the air can perch in its shade.

The kingdom of God is like yeast that a woman mixed into 60 pounds of flour until it spread throughout the dough.

The kingdom of heaven is like treasure hidden in a field. The man who found it hid it again. Filled with joy, he sold all he had and purchased the field.

The kingdom of heaven is like a merchant searching for fine pearls. He found one of great value and sold everything he had to buy it.

The kingdom of heaven is like a net cast into the lake. It caught all kinds of fish and when it was full, the fishermen pulled it ashore. Then they sat down and collected the good fish in baskets but threw the bad away. This is how it will be at the end of the age. The angels will separate the wicked from the righteous and throw them into the fiery furnace, where there will be weeping and gnashing of teeth.

The Parable of the Wheat and the Weeds
MT 13:24-30|MT 13:34-35|MK 4:33-34

The kingdom of heaven is like a man who planted good seed in his field. But an enemy planted weeds among the wheat while everyone was sleeping, and then he slipped away. When the plants grew and began to ripen, the weeds became visible too.

The owner's servants said, "Sir, didn't you plant good seed? Where did the weeds come from?"

"An enemy planted them," he replied.

"Should we pull them up?"

"No, you might pull up the wheat while pulling the weeds. Let them both grow together until the harvest. I'll instruct the harvesters to gather the weeds and tie them in bundles to be burned, but they'll gather the wheat and bring it into my barn."

Jesus taught the crowd nothing without parables, teaching them as much as they could understand. But he explained everything when he was alone with his disciples.

This fulfilled what the prophet spoke: *I will open my mouth in parables; I will speak things hidden since the creation of the world.*

Jesus Explains Why He Speaks in Parables
MT 13:10-17|MT 13:36a|MK 4:10-12|MK 4:25|LK 8:10|LK 8:18

After Jesus dismissed the crowd and went into the house, the Twelve asked him, "Why do you speak to the people in parables?"

He replied, "I'm giving you knowledge of the secrets of the kingdom of heaven, but I speak in parables to those on the outside. Therefore, consider carefully how you listen. Whoever has will be given more, and he will have an abundance. Whoever doesn't have, even what he has will be taken from him. When I speak in parables, Isaiah's prophecy is fulfilled: *They will listen and listen but never hear or understand; they will look and look but never really see. They're so stubborn that they've stopped up their ears and closed their eyes. If they could hear with their ears, see with their eyes, or understand with their minds, they would turn to God and be forgiven!*

"But blessed are your eyes because they see, and your ears because they hear. I assure you, many prophets and righteous men longed to see what you see, but they didn't see it, and to hear what you hear, but they didn't hear it."

"Explain the parable of the weeds in the field," his disciples replied.

"The one who sowed the good seed is the Son of Man. The field is the world, and the good seed represents the sons of the kingdom. The weeds are the sons of the evil one, and the enemy who sows them is the devil. The harvest is the end of the age, and the harvesters are angels.

"Just as the weeds are pulled up and burned in the fire, so it will be at the end of the age. The Son of Man will send his angels to weed out of his kingdom everything that causes sin and everyone who does evil. They will throw them into the fiery furnace, where there will be weeping and gnashing of teeth. Then the righteous will shine like the sun in the kingdom of their Father. He who has ears, let him hear. Do you understand?"

"Yes," they replied.

"Every teacher of the law who's been instructed about the kingdom of heaven is like the owner of a house who brings both new and old treasures out of his storeroom."

When Jesus finished these parables, he departed from that place.

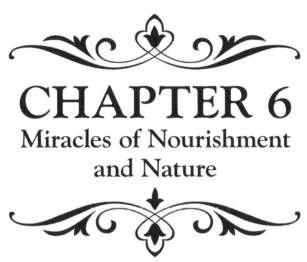

CHAPTER 6
Miracles of Nourishment and Nature

Jesus Calms the Storm
MT 8:18|MT 8:23-27|MK 4:35-41|LK 8:22-25

That evening Jesus said to his disciples, "Let's cross over to the other side."

Some boats were there, and Jesus was already in one of them, so they took him in it just as he was. A violent storm arose, causing the waves to overtake the boat so that it was nearly swamped, and they were in great danger.

But Jesus was in the back of the boat sleeping on a cushion.

The disciples woke him and said, "Lord, save us! Don't you care if we die?"

"You have so little faith," he said. "Why are you afraid?"

Then he got up and rebuked the wind and he said to the waves, "Quiet! Be still!"

The wind died down and it was completely calm.

"What kind of man is this?" the disciples asked each other in fear and amazement. "He commands even the winds and the sea, and they obey him!"

Jesus Heals Two Demon-Possessed Men
MT 8:28-34|MK 5:1-20|LK 8:26-39

They sailed to the region of Gerasa and Gadara, which is across the lake from Galilee. Two demon-possessed men had lived there for a long time, naked among the tombs.

They were chained hand and foot and kept under guard, but still the demon constantly seized them, tore the chains apart, and broke the irons. No one could bind them and no one was strong enough to subdue them.

The demon had driven them into solitary places among the tombs and in the hills. They cried out night and day and cut themselves with stones. They were so violent that no one could pass that way.

When Jesus stepped ashore, the two demon-possessed men saw him from a distance and ran from the tombs to meet him, falling to their knees in front of him, shouting, "What do you want, Jesus, Son of the Most High God? Did you come to torture us before the appointed time?" And they begged him repeatedly not to cast them into hell's bottomless pit.

"What's your name?" Jesus asked.

"Our name is Legion, for we are many."

"Come out, you evil spirit!" Jesus commanded.

About 2000 pigs were feeding on the hillside nearby, so the demons begged Jesus, "Allow us to enter the pigs."

He gave them permission, and the demons left the men and went into the pigs. The herd rushed down the steep bank into the lake and drowned.

Then those tending the pigs ran off into the city and the countryside and reported what had happened to the pigs and the demon-possessed men.

So everyone throughout the region went to see Jesus and found the formerly possessed men sitting at Jesus' feet, dressed and in their right mind. The people were afraid and begged Jesus to leave their region.

As Jesus was getting into the boat, the formerly possessed men begged to go with him.

But Jesus said, "Go home to your family. Tell them how much the Lord has done for you and how he had mercy on you."

So they told everyone in the Decapolis and everyone was amazed.

Jesus Raises a Dead Girl and Heals a Sick Woman
MT 9:1|MT 9:18-26|MK 5:21-43|LK 8:40-56

When Jesus returned by boat to the other side of the lake, a large crowd was waiting and they welcomed him.

A man named Jairus, a ruler of the synagogue, fell at Jesus' feet and pleaded earnestly with him because his only daughter, who was about 12, was near death. "My little daughter is dying. Please come touch her and heal her so she won't die."

Jesus and his disciples went with him, and the crowd followed so closely they almost crushed Jesus. A woman was there who had been bleeding for 12 years and suffered greatly. She had been under the care of many doctors and spent all she had, yet she continued to get worse. When she heard about Jesus, she came up behind him in the crowd and touched the edge of his robe because she thought, *I'll be healed if I can touch even the edge of his clothing.* Immediately her bleeding stopped and she felt in her body that she was freed from her suffering.

Jesus turned around and asked, "Who touched me?"

When they all denied it, Peter said, "Master, how can you ask that when all these people are pressing against you?"

"I know someone touched me because power has gone out from me." And he kept looking around to see who had done it.

The woman realized she couldn't remain hidden, so she came forward and fell at Jesus' feet. Trembling with fear, she told him in the presence of everyone the whole truth about why she had touched him and how she had been instantly healed.

"Have courage, daughter," Jesus said, "your faith has healed you. Go in peace and be freed from your suffering."

While Jesus was still speaking, someone came from Jairus' house and said, "Your daughter is dead. Don't bother the teacher anymore."

Jesus heard him and said to Jairus, "Don't be afraid. Believe and she will be healed."

He didn't let anyone follow him except Peter, James, and his brother John.

When Jesus entered the ruler's house and saw the flute players and the crowd crying and mourning, he said, "Why are you making all this noise? Don't cry, the child isn't dead, but asleep."

They laughed at him because they knew she was dead.

Jesus put them all out, taking only the child's parents and his three disciples in with him. Then he took her hand and said, *"Talitha koum!"* (which means *Little girl, get up!*).

Her spirit returned and immediately she stood up and walked around. Then Jesus told them to give her something to eat. Her parents were amazed, but he ordered them not to tell anyone about what happened. However, the news still spread throughout that region.

Jesus Sends Out the Twelve
MT 9:35|MT 9:37-38|MT 10:1|MT 10:5-33
MT 10:37-42|MT 11:1|MK 6:6b-13|LK 6:40
LK 9:1-6|LK 10:2-12|LK 12:2-9|LK 12:11-12

Jesus traveled through all the cities and villages, teaching in their synagogues, preaching the good news of the kingdom, and healing every sickness and disease.

He said to his disciples, "The harvest is plentiful but the workers are few. Ask the Lord of the harvest to send workers into his harvest field."

Then he gave them power and authority to drive out all demons and to cure diseases, sending them out two by two to preach the kingdom of God.

These were his instructions: "Don't go to Gentile or Samaritan cities. Instead, go to the lost sheep of Israel and preach, 'The kingdom of heaven is near.' Heal the sick, raise the dead, cleanse those who have leprosy, and cast out demons. You have received freely, now freely give. Don't take any gold, silver, or copper in your belts. Don't take a bag, an extra shirt, extra sandals, or an extra staff for the journey, and don't greet anyone on the road.

"When you visit a house say, 'Peace upon this house.' If a man of peace is there, your peace will rest on him; if not, it will return to you. Then search for a worthy person in that city and stay at his house until you leave. Don't move around from house to house. Eat and drink whatever you are given, for the worker deserves his pay. Heal the sick there and tell them, 'The kingdom of God is near you.'

"But when you enter a city and aren't welcomed, go into the streets and say, 'We wipe off against you even the dust of your city that sticks to our feet. You can be sure of this: the kingdom of God is near.' I assure you, it will be more bearable for Sodom and Gomorrah on judgment day than it will be for that city.

"I'm sending you out like sheep among wolves. Therefore, be as shrewd as snakes and as innocent as doves. Be wary of men — they will hand you over to the local councils and flog you in their synagogues. Because of me, you will be brought before governors and kings as witnesses to them and to the Gentiles. But when they arrest you and bring you before synagogues, rulers, and authorities, don't worry about how you will defend yourselves; the Holy Spirit will teach you what to say at that time.

"Brother will betray brother to death, and a father his child; children will rebel against their parents and have them put to death. All men will hate you because of me, but he who stands firm to the end will be saved. When they persecute you in one place, flee to another. I assure you, you won't have visited all the cities of Israel before the Son of Man comes.

"A student isn't above his teacher, nor a servant above his master, but everyone who is fully trained will be like his teacher. If they called the head of the house Beelzebub, they're more likely to do the same to the members of his household. But don't be afraid of them. Nothing is concealed that won't be revealed, or hidden that won't be made known. What

I tell you in the dark, speak in the daylight; what is whispered in your ear, in the inner rooms, proclaim from the rooftops.

"My friends, don't be afraid of those who kill the body but can't kill the soul. Instead, fear him who, after killing the body, has the power to destroy both soul and body in hell. Yes, I tell you, fear him. Aren't two sparrows sold for a penny? Yet not one of them will fall to the ground unless it's your Father's will. Even the very hairs of your head are numbered, so don't be afraid — you're worth more than many sparrows.

"I'll acknowledge before my Father in heaven whoever acknowledges me before others. But I'll disown before my Father in heaven whoever disowns me before others. Anyone who loves his father or mother more than me isn't worthy of me; anyone who loves his son or daughter more than me isn't worthy of me; and anyone who doesn't take his cross and follow me isn't worthy of me. Whoever finds his life will lose it, and whoever loses his life because of me will find it. He who receives you receives me, and he who receives me receives the One who sent me. Anyone who receives a prophet because he is a prophet will receive a prophet's reward, and anyone who receives a righteous man because he is righteous will receive a righteous man's reward."

After Jesus finished instructing his disciples, he went to teach and preach in the cities of Galilee. And the disciples went from village to village preaching that people should repent. They drove out many demons and anointed many sick people with oil and healed them.

Herod Has John the Baptist Beheaded
MT 14:5-12|MK 6:18-29

Now Herodias held a grudge against John the Baptist. She wanted to have him killed because John had been telling Herod, "It's against the law for you to marry Herodias, your brother Philip's wife."

But she wasn't able to have him killed, because Herod feared John and protected him. He was afraid of the people because they considered John a prophet, and he knew John was a righteous and holy man. Herod was very confused when he heard John preach, yet he liked to listen to him.

Herod gave a banquet on his birthday for his high officials, military commanders, and the leading men of Galilee. Herodias' daughter came in and danced for them, and Herod and his dinner guests were pleased.

"Ask for anything you want and I'll give it to you, up to half my kingdom," the king promised her.

So she went and asked her mother, "What should I ask for?"

Finally Herodias saw an opportunity, so she said, "Ask for the head of John the Baptist."

Immediately the girl hurried in to the king and said, "Give me right now John the Baptist's head on a platter."

This upset the king very much, but he didn't want to refuse her because he had made the promise in front of his dinner guests. So Herod immediately sent an executioner to the prison. He beheaded John, brought back his head on a platter, and gave it to the girl, who then gave it to her mother.

When John's disciples heard what happened, they took his body and laid it in a tomb. Then they went to tell Jesus.

Jesus Feeds the 5000
MT 9:36|MT 14:13-23|MK 6:30-46
MK 9:38-41|LK 9:10-17|LK 9:49-50|JN 6:1-15

Meanwhile the apostles returned from their mission and reported to Jesus everything they had done and taught.

"Master," John said, "we saw a man driving out demons in your name and we tried to stop him because he isn't one of us."

"Don't stop him," Jesus said. "No one who does a miracle in my name can in the next moment say anything bad about me. Whoever isn't against us is for us. I assure you, anyone who gives even a cup of cold water to any of these little ones because he is my disciple will certainly not lose his reward."

After hearing about John the Baptist's death, Jesus said to his disciples, "Come with me to a quiet place where we can rest."

So many people were coming and going that they didn't even have a chance to eat. So they traveled in a boat to a secluded place in Bethsaida, crossing to the far shore of the Sea of Galilee (also called the Sea of Tiberias) to Bethsaida.

Many people saw them leaving and recognized them because they had seen Jesus miraculously heal the sick. So they ran on foot from all the cities and arrived at Bethsaida before them.

Jesus felt compassion when he landed and saw the crowds. They were weary and helpless, like sheep without a shepherd. He went up on a mountainside and sat down with his disciples. The Jewish Passover Feast was near. He welcomed the people and spoke to them about the kingdom of God, teaching them many things. And he healed those who needed healing.

By this time it was late in the afternoon, and the Twelve said to Jesus, "Send the crowd away so they can find food and lodging in the surrounding villages and countryside. This is a remote place and it's already very late."

Jesus replied, "They don't need to leave." Then he asked Philip, "Where should we buy bread for these people?" He asked this only to test him, for he already knew what he was going to do.

"Eight months' wages wouldn't buy enough bread for each one to have a bite!" Philip said. "Surely we're not going to spend that much to try to feed them all?"

"You give them something to eat," Jesus said. "Go see how many loaves of bread you have."

Andrew, Simon Peter's brother, said, "A boy has five small barley loaves and two small fish, but how far will they go among so many?"

"Bring them here."

Then Jesus directed his disciples to sit the people down on the green grass in groups of hundreds and fifties. Looking toward heaven, he gave thanks. Then he broke the five loaves and the two fish into pieces. He gave them to his disciples, who distributed to the people as much as they wanted.

When everyone had enough to eat, Jesus said to his disciples, "Gather the leftovers so nothing is wasted."

So they filled 12 baskets with the rest of the broken pieces of bread and fish. About 5000 men had eaten, not counting women and children.

Afterward the people said, "Surely this is the Prophet who was to come into the world."

Jesus knew they intended to make him king by force, so he immediately made the disciples get into the boat and cross to the other side to Capernaum. He dismissed the crowd and then he went up the mountainside by himself to pray.

Jesus Walks on Water
MT 14:24-36|MK 6:47-56|JN 6:16-24

The disciples set off across the lake for Capernaum, and when it grew dark, Jesus still hadn't joined them. The boat was already a considerable distance from land, tossed by the waves because the wind beat against it.

Jesus saw that the disciples were having trouble rowing. Around 3am they had rowed about three and a half miles, and they saw Jesus walking on the water toward the boat. He was about to pass by them.

"It's a ghost!" they shouted, terrified.

"Take courage," Jesus said. "It is I. Don't be afraid."

"Lord, if it's you, tell me to come to you on the water," Peter said.

"Come."

So Peter got out of the boat and walked on the water toward Jesus. But he saw the wind and was afraid, so he began to sink. "Lord, save me!" he cried out.

Jesus quickly caught him. "You have so little faith," he said. "Why did you doubt?"

The wind died down when they got back into the boat, and the other disciples worshiped Jesus, saying, "You truly are the Son of God."

They were completely amazed because they hadn't understood the miracle of the loaves; their hearts were hardened.

Immediately the boat reached the shore at Gennesaret, and they anchored there. People recognized Jesus as soon as they got out of the boat. They ran throughout that whole region and carried the sick to him on mats. And wherever he went — into villages, cities, or the countryside — they placed the sick in the marketplaces, begging him to let them touch even the edge of his robe, and everyone who touched him was healed.

The next day on the opposite shore, where the Lord had given thanks and fed the 5000, the crowd realized that Jesus and his disciples were no longer there. They had seen only one boat, but Jesus' disciples had left in it without him. Then some boats from Tiberias docked near that place, so they got in the boats and sailed to Capernaum to look for Jesus.

Jesus Is the Bread of Life
JN 6:25-59

They found Jesus on the other side of the lake in Capernaum, teaching at the synagogue. "Rabbi, when did you get here?" they asked.

Jesus said, "You're looking for me because you ate the loaves and were filled, not because you saw miraculous signs. Don't work for food that spoils but for food that endures to eternal life, which the Son of Man will give you. God the Father has placed his seal of approval on him."

"What kind of work does God require?" they asked.

"The work of God is to believe in the one he sent."

They replied, "The scriptures say, *He gave them bread from heaven to eat.* Our forefathers ate manna in the desert, but what miraculous sign will you perform so we can believe in you?

"Moses gave you bread from heaven," Jesus said, "but I assure you, my Father is the one who gives you the true bread from heaven. The bread of God is he who comes down from heaven and gives life to the world."

"Sir," they said, "Give us this bread from now on."

"I am the bread of life. He who comes to me will never go hungry and he who believes in me will never be thirsty. I told you before, but even though you've seen me, you still don't believe. Everyone that the Father gives me will come to me, and whoever comes to me I'll never drive away. I came down from heaven not to do my will, but to do the will of the one who sent me. And his will is that I lose none of those he gave me but raise them up at the last day. My Father's will is that everyone who looks to the Son and believes in him will have eternal life, and I'll raise him up at the last day."

The Jews protested because he referred to himself as bread from heaven. "Isn't this Jesus the son of Joseph, whose father and mother we know? How can he say he came down from heaven?"

"Stop grumbling," Jesus said. "No one can come to me unless the Father who sent me draws him, and I'll raise him up at the last day. It is written in the Prophets: *They will all be taught by God.* Everyone who listens to the Father and learns from him comes to me. No one has seen the Father except the one who is from God; only he has seen the Father. I assure you, he who believes has everlasting life.

"I am the bread of life. Your ancestors ate manna in the desert and they died. But I am the bread that comes down from heaven, which a man can eat and not die. Anyone who eats of this bread will live forever. This bread is my flesh, which I'll give for the life of the world."

The Jews argued passionately among themselves, asking, "How can he give us his flesh to eat?"

"I assure you," Jesus said, "unless you eat the flesh of the Son of Man and drink his blood, you have no life in you. Whoever eats my flesh and drinks my blood has eternal life, and I'll raise him up at the last day. My flesh is real food and my blood is real drink. Whoever eats my flesh and drinks my blood remains in me, and I in him. Just as the living Father sent me and I live because of the Father, so the one who feeds on me will live because of me. This is the bread that came down from heaven. Your forefathers ate manna and died, but he who feeds on this bread will live forever."

Many Disciples Desert Jesus
JN 6:60-71|JN 7:1

Many of his followers said, "How can we accept this teaching? It's too difficult!"

Jesus heard them and said, "Does this offend you? What if you see the Son of Man ascend to where he was before? The Spirit gives life — the flesh counts for nothing. The words I spoke are spirit and life, but some of you don't believe. That's why I said no one can come to me unless the Father enables him."

Jesus knew from the beginning which of them didn't believe and who would betray him.

From then on, many people refused to continue following him.

"Do you want to leave too?" Jesus asked the Twelve.

"Lord, to whom would we go?" Simon Peter asked. "You have the words of eternal life. We believe, and we know that you are the Holy One of God."

Jesus replied, "I chose the Twelve of you, but one of you is a devil!"

He was referring to Judas, the son of Simon Iscariot, who would soon betray him.

Jesus traveled throughout Galilee, purposely staying away from Judea because the Jews there were waiting to kill him.

Herod Tries to See Jesus
MT 14:1-2|MK 6:14-16|LK 9:7-9

Because Jesus' name had become so well-known, Herod the tetrarch heard the reports about him. He was confused because some people said he was John, raised from the dead. Others said he was Elijah or a prophet like those long ago.

Herod said to his attendants, "Who is this man everyone is talking about? I beheaded John the Baptist but it must be John! He has such miraculous powers because he has risen from the dead!"

So he tried to see Jesus.

Jesus Teaches About What Makes One Unclean
MT 15:1-20|MK 7:1-23|LK 6:39

Now the Pharisees and Jews ceremonially wash their hands before eating and when they come from the marketplace, in accordance with the tradition of the elders. They also observe many other traditions, such as the washing of cups, pitchers, and kettles.

The Pharisees and teachers of the law came from Jerusalem and gathered around Jesus. They saw some of his disciples eating food with unclean hands, so they asked Jesus, "Why do your disciples break the tradition of the elders? They don't wash their hands before they eat!"

Jesus replied, "You yourself set aside God's commands in favor of observing your own traditions! God said, *Honor your father and mother* and *Anyone who curses his father or mother must be put to death.* But if a man designates something as a gift dedicated to God (called *Corban*), you encourage him to make that a priority instead of helping his parents. In this and many other ways, you invalidate the word of God by your tradition.

"You hypocrites! Isaiah was right when he prophesied about you: *These people honor me with their lips, but their hearts are far from me. They worship me in vain; their teachings are but rules taught by men.*"

Jesus then addressed the crowd, "Everyone listen to me and understand this. Nothing that enters a man from the outside can make him unclean. Rather, it's what comes out of a man that makes him unclean."

After he left the crowd and entered the house, the disciples asked, "Do you know that the Pharisees were offended by what you said?"

Jesus replied, "Every plant that my heavenly Father hasn't planted will be pulled up by the roots. Don't worry about them — they are blind guides. Can a blind man lead a blind man? Won't they both fall into a pit?"

"Explain the parable to us," Peter asked.

"You still don't understand that nothing that enters a man from the outside can make him unclean? It doesn't go into his heart but into his stomach, and then out of his body." (By saying this, Jesus declared all foods clean.) He continued, "But what comes out of the mouth comes from the heart, and these things make a man unclean. For out of the heart come evil thoughts, murder, adultery, sexual immorality, theft, false testimony, slander, greed, malice, deceit, lewdness, envy, arrogance, and folly. All these evils come from within and make a man unclean, but eating with unwashed hands doesn't make him unclean."

A Gentile Woman Has Faith
MT 15:21-30|MK 7:24-31

One day Jesus was staying in a house in the region of Tyre. He didn't want anyone to know he was there but couldn't keep his presence secret.

A Canaanite woman from that area heard about him and went to see him. She was a Greek, born in Syrian Phoenicia. "Lord, Son of David, have mercy on me!" she cried out. "My daughter is suffering terribly from demon possession."

When Jesus didn't respond, his disciples urged him, "Help her and send her away; she keeps crying out after us."

"I was sent only to the lost sheep of Israel," Jesus said to them.

Then the woman came and fell at his feet, "Lord, help me!" And she kept asking him to drive out the demon.

"First let the children eat all they want," he replied. "It's not right to take the children's bread and toss it to their dogs."

"Yes Lord," she replied, "but even the dogs under the table eat the children's crumbs."

"Woman, you have great faith! Your request is granted and the demon has left your daughter."

And she went home and found her child lying on the bed, free of the demon.

Jesus left Tyre and traveled through Sidon, down to the Sea of Galilee and into the region of the Decapolis. He went up on a mountainside and sat down. Great crowds brought the lame, blind, crippled, mute, and many others. They laid them all at Jesus' feet and he healed them.

Jesus Heals a Deaf Mute
MT 15:31|MK 7:32-37

One of those brought to Jesus was a deaf man with a speech impediment, and they begged him to heal the man.

Jesus took him away from the crowd and put his fingers into his ears. Then he spit and put the saliva on the man's tongue. He looked up to heaven and said with a deep sigh, *"Ephphatha!"* (This means, *Be opened!*)

The man's ears opened, his tongue loosened, and he spoke clearly.

The people were amazed when they saw the mute speaking, the crippled made well, the lame walking, and the blind seeing. And they praised the God of Israel. "He does everything well," they said. "He even makes the deaf hear and the mute speak."

Jesus commanded them not to tell anyone. But the more he did so, the more they kept talking about it.

Jesus Feeds the 4000
MT 15:32-38|MK 8:1-9a

During those days another large crowd gathered. Jesus said to his disciples, "I have compassion for these people; they've already been with me three days and have nothing to eat. Some of them have traveled a long distance and if I send them home hungry, they'll faint on the way."

"Where could we get enough bread in this remote place to feed such a crowd?" his disciples asked.

"How many loaves do you have?" Jesus asked.

"Seven," they replied, "and a few small fish."

So Jesus told the crowd to sit on the ground. He gave thanks and broke the seven loaves and the fish and gave them to the disciples. They distributed the food and everyone ate and was satisfied. Afterward the disciples collected seven basketfuls of leftover pieces. Four thousand men had eaten, besides women and children.

The Jewish Leaders Demand a Sign
MT 15:39|MT 16:1-4|MK 8:9b-13|LK 12:1a|LK 12:54-56

So many people were there that they were trampling over each other. Jesus sent the crowd away and took the boat to the vicinity of Magadan, in the region of Dalmanutha. The Pharisees and Sadducees visited Jesus and tested him, asking him to show them a sign from heaven.

He replied, "When evening comes you say, *'The sky is red so we'll have good weather'* and in the morning, *'Today the sky is red and overcast so it will be stormy.'* When the south wind blows you say, *'It's going to be hot'* and it is. Hypocrites! You know how to interpret the appearance of the earth and the sky. Why don't you know how to interpret the signs of the times? A wicked and adulterous generation looks for a miraculous sign, but none will be given it except the sign of Jonah."

Jesus then returned to the boat to cross to the other side.

Jesus Warns Against the Teaching of the Pharisees
MT 16:5-12|MK 8:14-21|LK 12:1b

As they crossed the lake, Jesus said to his disciples, "Be careful. Guard yourself against the yeast of the Pharisees, Sadducees, and Herod."

They only had one loaf with them in the boat and had forgotten to bring more. They discussed this among themselves: "He's saying that because we have no bread."

Jesus was aware of their discussion and said, "You have so little faith — why are you talking about having no bread? Do you still not understand? Are your hearts hardened? Do you have eyes but fail to see and ears but fail to hear? Don't you remember when I broke the five loaves for the 5000? How many basketfuls of leftovers did you collect?"

"Twelve," they replied.

"And how many basketfuls did you collect when I broke the seven loaves for the 4000?"

"Seven."

Then why don't you understand that I wasn't talking about bread? The yeast I spoke of is the hypocrisy of the Pharisees and Sadducees."

Then they understood that he wasn't telling them to beware of the yeast used in bread, but of the teaching of the Pharisees and Sadducees.

Jesus Heals a Blind Man at Bethsaida
MK 8:22-26

When they arrived in Bethsaida, some people brought a blind man to Jesus and begged him to heal the man.

Jesus took the blind man's hand and led him outside the village. He spit on his eyes, touched them, and asked, "Do you see anything?"

He looked up and said, "I see people who look like trees walking around."

Jesus touched the man's eyes again. His sight was restored and he saw everything clearly.

Jesus sent him home, saying, "Don't go into the village."

Peter Acknowledges Jesus as the Christ
MT 16:13-20|MK 8:27-30|LK 9:18-21

Jesus and his disciples traveled throughout the villages around Caesarea Philippi.

After praying in private, Jesus asked his disciples, "Who do people say that I, the Son of Man, am?"

"Some say John the Baptist," they replied. "Others say Elijah, Jeremiah, or one of the prophets of long ago has come back to life."

"But what about you? Who do you say I am?"

Simon Peter said, "You are the Christ, the Son of the living God."

"You are blessed, Simon, son of Jonah. This wasn't revealed to you by man but by my Father in heaven. You are Peter and on this rock I will build my church, and the forces of hell will not overcome it. I'll give you the keys of the kingdom of heaven — whatever you bind on earth will be bound in heaven and whatever you loose on earth will be loosed in heaven."

Then Jesus warned his disciples not to tell anyone that he was the Christ.

Jesus Predicts His Death and Resurrection
MT 16:21-28|MK 8:31-38|MK 9:1|LK 9:22-27

From that time on, Jesus began teaching his disciples, saying, "The Son of Man must go to Jerusalem and suffer many things. He will be rejected by the elders, chief priests, and teachers of the law. He must be killed and will rise to life on the third day."

Peter pulled him aside and said, "No, Lord! This will never happen!"

Jesus turned to Peter and said, "Get behind me, Satan! You are a hindrance to me; you're not concerned about the things of God, but the things of men."

Then he gathered the crowd, along with his disciples, and said, "Anyone who wants to come after me must deny himself, take up his cross daily, and follow me. Whoever wants to save his life will lose it, but whoever loses his life for me and for the gospel will save it. What good is it for a man to gain the whole world but forfeit his soul? What can a man give that's worth exchanging his soul?

"If anyone is ashamed of me and my words in this adulterous and sinful generation, the Son of Man will be ashamed of him when he comes in his glory and in his Father's glory with the holy angels. Then he will reward each person according to what he has done. I assure you, some of you standing here won't taste death before seeing the kingdom of God come with power."

CHAPTER 7
The Transfiguration and Teachings

About a week later, Jesus took Peter, James, and John and led them up a high, secluded mountain. As he was praying, he was transformed. His face shone like the sun and his clothes turned a dazzling white, brighter than any launderer in the world could whiten them.

Suddenly, Moses and Elijah appeared in glorious splendor and spoke with Jesus about his death, which he was about to accomplish in Jerusalem.

Peter and his companions were very sleepy. When they were fully awake, they saw Jesus in all his glory and the two men standing with him.

As the men were leaving, Peter said, "Master, it's good that we're here. Let's build three shelters — one for you, one for Moses, and one for Elijah."

They were all very afraid and Peter didn't know what to say.

While he was still speaking, a bright cloud enveloped them. A voice from the cloud said, "This is my beloved Son, who pleases me very much. Obey him, for I have chosen him."

The disciples fell facedown to the ground, terrified.

But Jesus touched them and said, "Get up — don't be afraid."

When they looked up, they saw no one except Jesus.

The next day as they were coming down the mountain, Jesus instructed them, "Don't tell anyone about what you saw until the Son of Man has been raised from the dead."

They discussed among themselves what "rising from the dead" meant.

Then they asked Jesus, "Why do the teachers of the law say Elijah must come first?"

"Elijah will surely come first and restore all things. But I assure you, Elijah already came and they didn't recognize him. Instead, they did everything they wished to him. In the same way, the Son of Man is going to suffer at their hands."

The disciples then understood that he was talking about John the Baptist. And they told no one at that time about all they had seen.

Jesus Heals a Boy of an Evil Spirit
MT 17:14-21|MK 9:14-29|LK 9:37-43a|LK 17:5-6

They joined the other disciples and saw a large crowd surrounding them. And the teachers of the law were arguing with the disciples. The people were overwhelmed with wonder as soon as they saw Jesus, and they ran to greet him.

"What are you arguing about?" Jesus asked his disciples.

Then a man approached Jesus and knelt before him. "Teacher, I beg you to look at my son and have mercy on him. He's my only child. He's possessed by an evil spirit that has robbed him of speech. He screams whenever it seizes him; it throws him into convulsions, causing him to foam at the mouth, grind his teeth, and become stiff. It rarely leaves him and is destroying him. I asked your disciples to cast out the spirit, but they couldn't."

"You unbelieving and perverse generation," Jesus replied, "how long will I stay with you? How long will I put up with you? Bring your son here."

So they brought him. As he approached, the spirit saw Jesus and immediately threw the boy into convulsions. He fell to the ground and rolled around, foaming at the mouth.

Jesus asked the boy's father, "How long has he been like this?"

"Since he was a little boy. It often throws him into fire or water to kill him. But if you can do anything, take pity on us and help us."

"'If'? Everything is possible for those who believe."

Immediately the boy's father cried out, "Lord, I do believe — help me overcome my unbelief!"

Jesus saw the crowd running toward them, so he said, "You deaf and mute spirit, I command you to come out and never enter him again!"

The spirit shrieked, shook the boy violently, and came out.

The boy was so still that many said, "He's dead."

But Jesus took his hand, lifted him to his feet, and gave him back to his father.

And everyone was amazed at the greatness of God.

While everyone was marveling at all that Jesus did, he went indoors. His disciples asked him privately, "Why couldn't we drive the spirit out?"

"Because you have so little faith," Jesus said.

"Lord, increase our faith."

"I assure you, if you have faith as small as a mustard seed, you can say to this mountain, '*Move from here to there*' and it will move. You can say to this mulberry tree, '*Be uprooted and planted in the sea*' and it will obey you. Nothing will be impossible for you. But this kind of spirit can come out only by prayer."

Jesus Teaches About Prayer
MT 6:5-15|MT 7:7-11|MK 11:25-26|LK 11:1-13

One day when Jesus finished praying, one of his disciples asked, "Lord, teach us to pray as John taught his disciples."

"When you pray, don't be like the hypocrites," Jesus said. "They love to pray in the synagogues and on the street corners so others can see them. I assure you, they have received their reward in full. But when you pray, go into your room, close the door, and pray to your Father, who is unseen. Then your Father, who sees what is done in secret, will reward you. And when you pray, don't babble like the pagans, who think God will hear them because of their many words. Don't be like them — your Father knows what you need before you ask him.

"This is how you should pray: Our Father who dwells in heaven, may your name be honored as holy. May your kingdom come, and may your will be done on earth as it is in heaven. Give us each day our daily sustenance. And forgive us our sins, because we forgive those who sin against us. And lead us not into temptation, but deliver us from the evil one. For yours is the kingdom, and the power, and the glory forever. Amen.

"If you are angry with anyone when you pray, forgive him. If you forgive those who sin against you, your heavenly Father will also forgive you. But if you don't forgive their sins, your Father won't forgive your sins.

"Suppose someone visits a friend at midnight and says, 'Lend me three loaves of bread. A friend traveled to visit me and I have nothing to feed him.'

'Leave me alone,' the one inside answers, 'I've already locked the door and my children are with me in bed. I can't get up to give you anything.'

"I assure you, even though he won't get up and give him the bread because he's his friend, he will give him as much as he needs because of his boldness. So keep asking and it will be given to you; keep searching and you will find; keep knocking and the door will be opened to you. For everyone who asks receives; he who searches finds; and the door will be opened to the one who knocks.

"Fathers, would you give your son a stone if he asks for bread? A snake if he asks for a fish? A scorpion if he asks for an egg? If you who are evil know how to give good gifts to your children, how much more will your Father in heaven give good gifts like the Holy Spirit to those who ask him?"

The Parable of the Persistent Widow
LK 18:1-8

Jesus then told his disciples a parable to demonstrate that they should always pray and never give up:

> A judge lived in a certain city and a widow there kept asking him, "Grant me justice against my enemy."

> He refused for a while. Finally he said, "I don't fear God or care about people, but this widow keeps bothering me! I'll make sure she receives justice so she won't eventually wear me out with her requests!"

"Listen to the unjust judge," Jesus continued. "Won't God bring about justice for those he has chosen, who cry out to him day and night? Will he keep putting them off? I assure you, he'll see that they get justice, and quickly! But when the Son of Man comes, will he find faith on the earth?"

Jesus Predicts His Death a Second Time
MT 17:22-23|MK 9:30-32|LK 9:43b-45

They left that place and passed through Galilee. Jesus was teaching his disciples, so he didn't want anyone to know where they were.

"The Son of Man is going to be betrayed into the hands of men," he said. "They will kill him and he will be raised to life on the third day."

The disciples were filled with grief, but they didn't understand what he meant, because the meaning was hidden from them. However, they were afraid to ask him about it.

Jesus Pays the Annual Temple Tax
MT 17:24-27|MK 9:33a

After Jesus and his disciples arrived in Capernaum, the collectors of the half-shekel tax asked Peter, "Does your teacher pay the temple tax?"

"Yes he does," Peter said.

When Peter entered the house, Jesus spoke first. "What do you think, Simon? Do the kings of the earth collect duty and taxes from their own sons or from others?"

"From others," Peter said.

"Then the sons are exempt," Jesus said. "But so that we don't offend them, go fish in the lake. Open the mouth of the first fish you catch and you will find a shekel coin. Use it to pay my tax and yours."

Jesus' Brothers Question Him
JN 7:2-9

When the Feast of Tabernacles was near, Jesus' brothers asked him, "Why don't you go to Judea so your followers can see your miracles? No one who wants to become a public figure acts in secret. Why don't you show yourself to the world?"

Even his own brothers didn't believe in him.

"The right time for me hasn't yet come — for you, any time is right," Jesus said. "The world can't hate you, but it hates me because I testify that what it does is evil. You go to the Feast. I'm not going yet."

So Jesus stayed in Galilee and his brothers left for the Feast.

Samaritans Oppose Jesus
LK 9:51-56|JN 7:10

As the time approached for Jesus to be taken up to heaven, he was determined to go to Jerusalem, not publicly but in secret.

He sent messengers ahead to a Samaritan village to get things ready for him, but the people there didn't welcome him, because he was going to Jerusalem.

So James and John asked, "Lord, do you want us to call fire down from heaven to destroy them?"

But Jesus rebuked them, and they went to another village.

The Cost of Following Jesus
MT 8:19-22|LK 9:57-62

As they continued on their way, a teacher of the law approached him and said, "Teacher, I'll follow you wherever you go."

Jesus replied, "Foxes have holes and the birds of the air have nests, but the Son of Man has no place to lay his head."

Jesus said to another man, "Follow me."

But the man replied, "Lord, first let me go and bury my father."

"Follow me and let the dead bury their own dead," Jesus said, "but you go and proclaim the kingdom of God."

Still another said, "I'll follow you, Lord, but first let me go back and say goodbye to my family."

"No one who puts his hand to the plow and looks back is fit for service in the kingdom of God," Jesus said.

PART III

JESUS' LATER
JUDEAN MINISTRY

CHAPTER 8
Jesus' Teachings at the Feasts

Jesus Attends the Feast of Tabernacles
JN 7:11-24

Now at the Feast of Tabernacles, the Jews were watching for Jesus, asking, "Where is he?"

Many in the crowds whispered about him. Some said, "He's a good man." Others replied, "No, he deceives the people." But no one said anything publicly about him because they were afraid of the Jewish leaders.

The Feast was halfway over when Jesus finally went to the temple courts to teach. The Jews were amazed and asked, "How does he know so much without having studied?"

Jesus said, "My teaching isn't my own. It comes from he who sent me. Anyone who does the will of God will find out whether my teaching comes from God or whether I speak on my own. He who speaks on his own does so to gain honor for himself, but he who works for the honor of the one who sent him is a man of truth — there's nothing false about him. Didn't Moses give you the law? Yet not one of you keeps it — why are you trying to kill me?"

"You're demon-possessed," they said. "Who's trying to kill you?"

"I performed one miracle and you're all amazed. Yet you circumcise a child on the Sabbath because Moses gave you circumcision (though it didn't actually come from Moses, but from the patriarchs). If you can circumcise a child on the Sabbath to prevent the law of Moses from being broken, why are you angry with me for healing the whole man on the Sabbath? Stop judging by mere appearances and judge correctly."

People Wonder If Jesus Is the Christ
JN 7:25-44

Some of the people of Jerusalem asked, "Isn't this the man the leaders are trying to kill? He's here speaking publicly but they aren't doing anything. Have they really concluded that he's the Christ? But we know where this man is from; when the Christ comes, no one will know where he's from."

Jesus was still teaching in the temple courts and cried out, "Yes, you know me and you know where I'm from. I'm not here on my own, but he who sent me is true. You don't know him, but I know him because he sent me and I came from him."

Then some of the people tried to seize him, but no one was able to lay a hand on him, because his time hadn't yet come.

But many in the crowd put their faith in him, saying, "When the Christ comes, will he perform more miracles than this man?"

The Pharisees heard the crowd whispering about Jesus, so the chief priests and the Pharisees sent for temple guards to arrest him.

Jesus said, "I'm with you for only a short time and then I'll return to the One who sent me. You will look for me but you won't find me. And where I'm going, you can't come."

The Jews asked each other, "Where will he go that we can't find him? Will he go to where our people live scattered among the Greeks and teach them? What does he mean?"

On the last and greatest day of the Feast, Jesus stood up and said in a loud voice, "Anyone who is thirsty should come to me and drink. Whoever believes in me, as the Scripture said, *Streams of living water will flow from within him.*"

Jesus was speaking about the Spirit, whom those who believed in him would later receive. The Spirit hadn't been given because Jesus hadn't yet been glorified.

Some of the people said, "Surely he is the Prophet."

Others said, "No, he is the Christ."

Still others asked, "How can the Christ come from Galilee? Doesn't the Scripture say he will come from David's family and from Bethlehem, the city where David lived?"

So the people were divided because of Jesus. Some wanted to seize him, but no one laid a hand on him.

Jesus Validates His Testimony
JN 8:12-29

Jesus spoke again, saying, "I am the light of the world. Whoever follows me will never walk in darkness but will have the light of life."

The Pharisees challenged him, "You're acting as your own witness, so your testimony isn't valid."

"My testimony is valid even if I testify on my own behalf," Jesus said. "I know where I came from and where I'm going. But you have no idea where I come from or where I'm going. You judge by human standards; I pass judgment on no one. But if I do judge, my decisions are right, because I'm not alone. I stand with the Father. Your own Law states that the testimony of two men is valid. I testify for myself; my other witness is the Father, who sent me."

"Where is your father?" they asked.

"You don't know me or my Father," Jesus replied. "If you knew me, you would know my Father also."

He said this while teaching in the temple area near the place where people gave their offerings. But no one seized him, because his time hadn't yet come.

Jesus said again, "I'm going away and you will look for me, but you will die in your sin. You can't come where I'm going."

The Jews asked, "Is he going to kill himself? Is that why he says we can't go where he's going?"

Jesus continued, "You are from below; I am from above. You are of this world; I am not of this world. You will indeed die in your sins if you don't believe I'm the one I claim to be."

"Who are you?" they asked.

"Just who I've been claiming all along," Jesus replied. "I have much to say in judgment of you. But he who sent me is reliable, and I tell the world what I've heard from him."

They didn't understand that he was telling them about his Father.

So Jesus said, "When you lift up the Son of Man, then you'll know that I'm the one I claim to be and I do nothing on my own. I speak just what the Father taught me. He who sent me is with me; he hasn't left me alone, because I always do what pleases him."

Jesus Is Greater Than Abraham
JN 7:53|JN 8:1|JN 8:30-59

Even as Jesus spoke, many put their faith in him. So Jesus said to those Jews, "If you hold to my teaching, you are really my disciples. Then you will know the truth and the truth will set you free."

"We are Abraham's descendants and have never been anyone's slaves," they said. "How can you say we will be set free?"

Jesus replied, "I assure you, everyone who sins is a slave to sin. Now a slave has no permanent place in the family, but a son belongs to it forever. So if the Son sets you free, you will be free indeed. I know you're Abraham's descendants, yet you're ready to kill me because you have no room for my word. I'm telling you what I've seen in the Father's presence, and you do what you've heard from your father."

"Abraham is our father," they said.

"If you were Abraham's children, you would do the things Abraham did. But you're determined to kill me, a man who told you the truth I was given from God. Abraham didn't do such things. You're doing the things your own father does."

"We aren't illegitimate children," they protested. "The only Father we have is God himself."

"If God were your Father, you would love me, because I came from God and now I'm here," Jesus said. "I didn't come on my own; he sent me. You don't understand me because you can't accept the truth. You belong to your father, the devil, and you want to carry out your father's desires. He was a murderer from the beginning, not holding to the truth, because there's no truth in him. When he lies, he speaks his native language; he is a liar and the father of lies. Yet I tell the truth and you don't believe me! Can any of you prove me guilty of sin? If I'm telling the truth, why don't you believe me? He who belongs to God hears what God says. The reason you don't hear is that you don't belong to God."

The Jews said, "We were right. You're a Samaritan and you're demon-possessed!"

"I'm not possessed by a demon," said Jesus, "but I honor my Father and you dishonor me. I'm not seeking glory for myself, but there is one who seeks it and he is the judge. I assure you, no one who keeps my word will ever see death."

"Now we know you're demon-possessed! Are you greater than our father Abraham? He died and so did the prophets, but you say no one who keeps your word will die. Who do you think you are?"

Jesus replied, "If I glorify myself, my glory means nothing. My Father, whom you claim as your God, is the one who glorifies me. You don't know him, but I do. If I said I didn't, I would be a liar like you. But I do know him and keep his word. Your father Abraham rejoiced that he would see my day; he saw it and was glad."

"How can you have seen Abraham when you aren't even 50 years old?" the Jews asked.

"I assure you, before Abraham was born, I Am!"

So they picked up stones to stone him but Jesus hid himself. Slipping away from the temple grounds, he went to the Mount of Olives.

Then everyone went home.

The Jewish Leaders Refuse to Believe
JN 7:45-52

The temple guards returned to the chief priests and Pharisees, who asked them, "Why didn't you bring him in?"

"No one ever spoke the way this man does," the guards said.

"You mean he deceived you too?" the Pharisees retorted. "Do we or the other rulers believe in him? No! But this mob, who knows nothing about the law, is cursed."

Nicodemus, who was also a Pharisee and had previously visited Jesus, asked, "Does our law condemn anyone without first allowing him to speak for himself about what he's doing?"

They replied, "Are you from Galilee, too? Check it out and you'll find that no prophet comes from Galilee."

Jesus Forgives an Adulterous Woman
JN 8:2-11

At dawn Jesus went to the temple courts again. The people gathered around him and he sat down to teach them.

Then the teachers of the law and the Pharisees brought in a woman and made her stand before the group. They said to Jesus, "Teacher, this woman was caught in the act of adultery. Moses commanded us in the Law to stone such women. Now what do you say?" They were trying to trap him so they'd have a reason to accuse him.

But Jesus bent down and began writing on the ground with his finger. When they kept questioning him, he straightened up and said, "Those of you without sin should be the first to throw a stone." Then he stooped down and wrote on the ground again.

So they left — one at a time, the older ones first — until only Jesus and the woman remained.

Jesus stood up and asked, "Woman, where are they? Has no one condemned you?"

"No one, Lord."

"Then I don't condemn you either. Go and leave your life of sin."

Jesus Heals a Man Born Blind
JN 9:1-41

One day Jesus saw a man who had been blind from birth. His disciples asked, "Rabbi, was he born blind because he sinned or because his parents sinned?"

"Neither this man nor his parents sinned," Jesus said, "but this happened so that the work of God could be displayed in his life. As long as it is day, we must do the work of the One who sent me. Night is coming, when no one can work. While I'm in the world, I am the light of the world."

Then he spit on the ground, made some mud with the saliva, put it on the man's eyes, and said, "Go wash in the Pool of Siloam." (Siloam means *sent*.)

The man went and washed his eyes and returned home seeing.

His neighbors and those who had seen him before asked, "Isn't this the same man who used to sit and beg?"

Some claimed that he was. Others said, "No, he only looks like him."

But he insisted, "I am the man."

"How are you able to see?" they demanded.

"The man they call Jesus made some mud and put it on my eyes. He told me to go to wash in Siloam. After I did, I could see."

"Where is this man?" they asked.

"I don't know."

So they brought him to the Pharisees, who asked him how he received his sight.

"A man put mud on my eyes and I washed them. Now I can see."

The day Jesus had healed him was a Sabbath, so some of the Pharisees said, "This man isn't from God; he doesn't keep the Sabbath."

But others asked, "How can a sinner perform such miracles?"

So they were divided.

Finally they asked the blind man, "What do you say about him? It was your eyes he opened."

"He's a prophet."

The Jews still didn't believe that he had been healed of his blindness, so they sent for his parents and asked, "Is this your son, the one you say was born blind? How can he now see?"

"He's our son," they said, "and we know he was born blind. But we don't know how he can see now or who opened his eyes. Ask him. He's old enough to speak for himself."

His parents said this because they were afraid of the Jews, who had decided that anyone who acknowledged Jesus as the Christ would be put out of the synagogue.

The Pharisees summoned the man who had been blind. "Give glory to God," they said. "We know the man who healed you is a sinner."

He replied, "I don't know whether he's a sinner or not. But one thing I do know — I was blind but now I can see!"

"What did he do to you?" they asked. "How did he open your eyes?"

"I told you already and you didn't listen. Why do you want to hear it again? Do you want to become his disciples too?"

They insulted him and said, "You're this fellow's disciple! We're disciples of Moses! We know God spoke to Moses, but we don't even know where this man comes from."

"Now that's remarkable!" the man said. "You don't know where he comes from, yet he opened my eyes. We know God doesn't listen to sinners. He listens to the godly man who does his will. Nobody ever heard of opening the eyes of a man born blind. If this man weren't from God, he could do nothing."

"You were born in total sin," they replied. "How dare you lecture us!"

Then they threw him out.

Jesus heard that they had thrown him out. When he found him, he asked, "Do you believe in the Son of Man?"

"Who is he, sir?" the man asked. "Tell me so I can believe in him."

Jesus said, "You have in fact now seen him. He's the one speaking with you now."

"Lord, I believe." And he worshiped Jesus.

Jesus said, "I've come into this world for judgment, so that the blind will see and those who see will become blind."

Some Pharisees heard him and asked, "So are we blind too?"

Jesus said, "You wouldn't be guilty of sin if you were blind, but since you claim you can see, your guilt remains."

Jesus Is the Good Shepherd
JN 10:1-21

"I assure you, the man who doesn't enter the sheep pen by the gate, but climbs in some other way, is a thief and a robber. The man who enters by the gate is the shepherd of his sheep. The guard opens the gate for him and the sheep listen to his voice. He calls his own sheep by name and leads out those belonging to him. He walks ahead of them and they follow him because they know his voice. They'll never follow a stranger; in fact, they'll run away from him because they don't recognize his voice."

Since Jesus was speaking figuratively, they didn't understand what he was telling them.

He continued, "I assure you, I am the gate for the sheep. All who came before me were thieves and robbers, but the sheep didn't listen to them. I am the gate — whoever enters through me will be saved. He will come in and then find pasture. The thief comes only to steal, kill, and destroy; I came that they may have life, and have it in abundance.

"I am the good shepherd who lays down his life for the sheep. The hired hand isn't the shepherd, who owns the sheep. So he abandons them and runs away when he sees the wolf coming, because he cares nothing for the sheep. So the wolf attacks the flock and scatters it.

"I am the good shepherd; I know my sheep and my sheep know me — just as the Father knows me and I know the Father — and I lay down my life for the sheep. I have other sheep that aren't of this sheep pen. I must bring them in also. They too will listen to my voice, and there will be one flock and one shepherd. My Father loves me because I am laying down my life so I can take it back again. No one takes it from me; I lay it down of my own accord. I have authority to lay it down and authority to take it back. I received this command from my Father."

The Jews were divided again. Many of them said, "He's demon-possessed and raving mad. Why listen to him?"

Others said, "He doesn't speak like a man possessed by a demon. Can a demon open the eyes of the blind?"

Jesus Sends Out the 72
LK 10:1|LK 10:17-20

Later, the Lord appointed 72 other disciples and sent them two by two ahead of him to every city and place where he was about to go. He gave them the same instructions he'd given when he had sent out the Twelve.

The 72 returned with joy and said, "Lord, even the demons submit to us in your name."

"I saw Satan fall like lightning from heaven," Jesus said. "I've given you authority to trample on snakes and scorpions and to overcome the power of the enemy; nothing will harm you. But don't rejoice that the spirits submit to you; rejoice that your names are written in heaven."

The Parable of the Good Samaritan
LK 10:25-37

On one occasion an expert in the law tested Jesus. "Teacher, what must I do to inherit eternal life?"

"What is written in the Law?" Jesus asked. "How do you read it?"

He said, *"Love the Lord your God with all your heart, with all your soul, with all your strength, and with all your mind and Love your neighbor as yourself."*

"You are correct," Jesus replied. "Do this and you will live."

But he wanted to justify himself so he asked, "Who is my neighbor?" And Jesus replied:

> A man was going down from Jerusalem to Jericho when robbers attacked him. They stripped him of his clothes, beat him, and left him half dead.
>
> A priest was traveling down the same road, but he passed by on the other side when he saw the man. A Levite also saw him and crossed to the other side.
>
> But a Samaritan saw him and took pity on him. He poured oil and wine on his wounds and bandaged them. Then he put the man on his donkey, brought him to an inn, and took care of him.
>
> The next day he gave the innkeeper two silver coins. "Take care of him," he said. "I'll reimburse you for any extra expense when I return."

"Which of these three do you think was a neighbor to the man who was robbed?" Jesus asked.

The expert in the law replied, "The one who showed him mercy."

"Then you go and do the same."

Jesus Visits Martha and Mary
LK 10:38-42

As Jesus and his disciples passed through a village, a woman named Martha opened her home to him. Her sister Mary sat at the Lord's feet listening to him, but Martha was distracted by all the preparations that had to be made.

"Lord," Martha said, "don't you care that Mary left me to do the work by myself? Tell her to help me!"

"Martha, Martha," the Lord said, "you're worried and upset about many things, but only one thing is needed. Mary has made the right choice and it won't be taken away from her."

Jesus Eats Dinner With a Pharisee
MT 23:25-28|LK 11:37-41|LK 11:44

One day a Pharisee invited Jesus to dinner. He was surprised when Jesus reclined at the table, because he noticed that Jesus didn't ritually wash before the meal.

So the Lord said, "You Pharisees clean the outside of the cup and dish, but inside you're full of greed and wickedness. You foolish people! Didn't the one who made the outside make the inside also? Give what is inside the dish to the poor and everything will be clean for you.

"You're like whitewashed tombs that men walk over without knowing it. They look beautiful on the outside but inside they're full of dead men's bones and everything unclean. In the same way, on the outside you appear to people as righteous but inside you're full of hypocrisy and wickedness. First clean the inside of the cup and dish, and then the outside will be clean as well."

The Parable of the Rich Fool
LK 12:13-21

One day someone in the crowd said, "Teacher, tell my brother to divide the inheritance with me."

Jesus replied, "Who appointed me as judge or intermediary between you? Watch out! Be on your guard against all kinds of greed; a man's life doesn't reside in the abundance of his possessions."

Then he told a parable:

A certain rich man's land produced a good crop. He thought, *I don't have a place to store my crops, so I'll tear down my barns and build bigger ones to store my grain and goods. Then I'll say to myself, "You have plenty of good things stored up for many years. Take life easy; eat, drink, and be merry."*

But God said, "You fool! This very night your life will be demanded from you. Then who will receive what you've prepared for yourself?"

"This is how it will be with anyone who stores up things for himself but isn't rich toward God," Jesus concluded.

Jesus Warns People to Repent or Perish
LK 13:1-9

Some people told Jesus about the Galileans whose blood Pilate had mixed with their sacrifices.

Jesus replied, "Do you think they were worse sinners than all the other Galileans because they suffered this way? Certainly not! What about the 18 who died when the tower in Siloam fell on them — do you think they were more guilty than everyone else living in Jerusalem? No! But unless you repent, all of you will perish too."

Then he told this parable:

> A man planted a fig tree in his vineyard. Some time later
> he went to look for fruit on it but didn't find any. So he said
> to the man who cared for his vineyard, "I've been coming
> to look for fruit on this fig tree for three years and haven't
> found any. Cut it down! Why should it use up the soil?"
>
> "Sir," the man replied, "leave it alone for one more year and
> give me a chance to dig around it and fertilize it. If it bears
> fruit next year, fine. If not, then you can cut it down."

Jesus Heals a Crippled Woman on the Sabbath
LK 13:10-17

One Sabbath Jesus was teaching in a synagogue. A spirit had crippled
a woman there for 18 years so that she was bent over and unable to stand
up straight.

Jesus called her forward and said, "Woman, you are set free from your
illness."

He touched her, and she immediately straightened up and praised
God.

The synagogue ruler was offended because Jesus had healed on the
Sabbath. He said to the people, "There are six days for work. Come be
healed on those days, not on the Sabbath."

Then the Lord said, "You hypocrites! On the Sabbath, don't you untie
your ox or donkey from the stall and take it out to give it water? Then
shouldn't this woman, a daughter of Abraham whom Satan kept bound
for 18 long years, be set free on the Sabbath?"

All his opponents were humiliated, but the people were delighted
with all the wonderful things he was doing.

Jewish Opposition at the Feast of Dedication
JN 10:22-39

It was winter and time for the Feast of Dedication in Jerusalem. And
Jesus was in the temple area walking in Solomon's Colonnade.

The Jews gathered around him and said, "How long will you keep us
in suspense? If you're the Christ, tell us plainly."

Jesus said, "I did tell you but you don't believe. The miracles I do in
my Father's name speak for me, but you don't believe because you aren't
my sheep. My sheep listen to my voice; I know them and they follow me.
I give them eternal life and they will never perish — no one can snatch
them out of my hand. My Father, who gave them to me, is greater than

all — no one can snatch them out of my Father's hand. I and the Father are one."

So the Jews picked up rocks to stone him.

"I've shown you many great miracles from the Father. For which of these do you stone me?" Jesus asked.

"Not for any of those reasons," the Jews replied, "but for blasphemy. You're a mere man, but you claim to be God."

"Isn't it written in your Law, *I have said you are gods?* If he called them "gods" to whom the word of God came — and the Scripture can't be broken — what about the one whom the Father set apart as his very own and sent into the world? Why do you accuse me of blasphemy because I said I'm God's Son? Don't believe me unless I do what my Father does. But if I do, then believe the miracles even though you don't believe me. And then you will know and understand that the Father is in me and I am in the Father."

Then they tried to seize him, but he escaped.

PART IV
JESUS' LATER
PEREAN MINISTRY

CHAPTER 9
The Perean Parables

Jesus Returns to Perea
JN 10:40-42

Then Jesus went back across the Jordan to the place where John had baptized in the early days. He stayed there a while and many people followed him.

"John never performed a miraculous sign, but everything he said about this man was true," they marveled.

So many people there believed in Jesus.

The Pharisees Warn Jesus
LK 13:31-33

At that time some Pharisees came to Jesus and said, "Leave and go somewhere else. Herod wants to kill you."

Jesus replied, "Go tell that fox, 'I'll drive out demons and heal people today and tomorrow, and on the third day I'll finish my work.' I must continue my travels today and tomorrow and the next day — because it's not proper for a prophet to die anywhere but in Jerusalem!"

Jesus Heals a Man on the Sabbath
LK 14:1-6

One Sabbath Jesus went to dinner at a prominent Pharisee's house, and everyone watched him carefully.

Jesus saw a man there whose body was swollen with fluid. So he asked the Pharisees and experts in the law, "Is it lawful to heal on the Sabbath or not?"

When they remained silent, Jesus took hold of the man, healed him, and sent him away.

Then he asked them, "If your son or ox falls into a well on the Sabbath, won't you immediately pull him out?"

But they had nothing to say.

A Parable of Humility
LK 14:7-14

When Jesus noticed that the guests chose the places of honor at the table, he told them this parable:

> When someone invites you to a wedding feast, don't take the place of honor, because the host may have invited a person more distinguished than you. Then he will say, "Give this man your seat." And you'll be humiliated and have to take the least important place. Instead, take the lowest place. Then your host will say, "Friend, move up to a better seat," and you'll be honored in the presence of your fellow guests. For everyone who exalts himself will be humbled, and he who humbles himself will be exalted.

Then Jesus said to his host, "When you give a luncheon or dinner, don't invite your friends, relatives, or rich neighbors. They will likely invite you back and so you'll be repaid. Instead, invite the poor, the crippled, the lame, and the blind and you will be blessed. Although they can't repay you, you'll be repaid at the resurrection of the righteous."

The Parable of the Great Banquet
LK 14:15-24

One of the men at the table said to Jesus, "Blessed is the man who will eat at the feast in the kingdom of God."

Jesus replied with a parable:

> A certain man prepared a great banquet and invited many guests. Then he sent his servant to tell the people, "Come, everything is ready."
>
> But they all made excuses. The first said, "I just bought a field and I must go and see about it. Please excuse me."
>
> Another said, "I just bought five yoke of oxen and I'm on my way to try them out. Please excuse me."
>
> Still another said, "I just got married so I can't come."
>
> The servant reported the responses to his master, the owner of the house. He was angry and ordered his servant, "Go out quickly into the city streets and alleys and bring in the poor, the crippled, the blind, and the lame."
>
> "Sir," the servant said, "I did what you asked, but there's still room."

"Then go out to the roads and country lanes and make the people come in so that my house will be full. I assure you, none of those I invited will taste my banquet."

The Cost of Discipleship
LK 14:25-33

Large crowds traveled with Jesus and he said to them, "No one who comes to me can be my disciple unless he hates his father and mother, his wife and children, his brothers and sisters — yes, even his own life. And no one can be my disciple unless he carries his cross and follows me."

Suppose one of you wants to build a tower. Won't he first sit down and estimate the cost to see if he has enough money to complete it? If he lays the foundation and isn't able to finish it, everyone will ridicule him, saying, "This fellow built and wasn't able to finish."

Or suppose a king is about to go to war against another king. Won't he first sit down and consider whether he is able with 10,000 men to oppose the one coming against him with 20,000? If he isn't able, he'll send a delegation while the other is still a long way off and ask for terms of peace.

"In the same way, no one who refuses to give up everything he owns can be my disciple."

The Parable of the Lost Sheep
MT 18:10-14|LK 15:1-7

When some tax collectors and sinners gathered around to listen to Jesus, the Pharisees and the teachers of the law mumbled, "This man welcomes sinners and eats with them!"

"Don't look down on these little ones," Jesus said. "I assure you that their angels in heaven always see the face of my Father in heaven. The Son of Man came to save those who were lost."

Then he told them this parable:

Suppose a man owns 100 sheep and one of them wanders away. Won't he leave the 99 in the open country and search for the lost sheep until he finds it? And then he will joyfully put it on his shoulders and go home and call his friends and neighbors together and say, "Rejoice with me; I found my lost sheep."

"I assure you, he is happier about that one sheep than about the 99 that didn't wander off. In the same way, there will be more rejoicing in heaven over one sinner who repents than over 99 righteous persons who don't need to repent. Your Father in heaven is not willing that any of these little ones should perish."

The Parable of the Lost Coin
LK 15:8-10

Or suppose a woman has ten silver coins and loses one. Doesn't she light a lamp, sweep the house, and search carefully until she finds it? She then calls her friends and neighbors together and says, "Rejoice with me; I found my lost coin."

"In the same way, God's angels rejoice over one sinner who repents."

The Parable of the Lost Son
LK 15:11-32

Jesus continued:

A man had two sons. The younger one said, "Father, give me my share of the estate."

So he divided his property between them.

Not long after that, the younger son gathered all he had and traveled to a distant country. There he lived recklessly and wasted his money. After he spent everything, a severe famine came upon that whole country and left him with nothing. So he went to work to feed pigs in someone's fields. He longed to fill his stomach with the pods that the pigs were eating, but no one gave him anything.

When he came to his senses, he said, "My father's hired men have food to spare, and here I am starving to death!" So he got up and traveled back home.

But while he was still a long way off, his father saw him and was filled with compassion for him. He ran to his son, threw his arms around him, and kissed him.

"Father, the son said, "I have sinned against heaven and against you. I'm no longer worthy to be called your son."

But the father said to his servants, "Quick! Dress him in the best robe. Put a ring on his finger and sandals on his feet. Kill the fattened calf so we can have a feast and celebrate. For my son was dead and is alive again; he was lost and now is found."

So they celebrated.

Meanwhile, the older son was out in the field. As he approached the house, he heard music and dancing, so he asked one of the servants what was going on.

"Your brother returned," he replied, "and your father killed the fattened calf to celebrate that he's back safe and sound."

The older brother was angry and refused to go in, so his father went out and pleaded with him.

But he said to his father, "Look! All these years I've been slaving for you and never disobeyed your orders. Yet you never gave me even a young goat so I could celebrate with my friends. But when this son of yours who squandered your money with prostitutes comes home, you kill the fattened calf for him!"

"My son, you're always with me and everything I have is yours. But we had to celebrate and be glad, because your brother was dead and now is alive again; he was lost and now is found."

The Parable of the Clever Manager
LK 16:1-16

One day Jesus told his disciples a parable:

A rich man received word that his manager was wasting his money. So he asked him, "What have you been doing? Turn in your final accounting records, because I'm relieving you of your position."

The manager thought, *What will I do now that I'm being fired? I'm not strong enough to dig and I'm ashamed to beg. I know! I'll arrange it so that when I lose my job here, people will welcome me into their houses.*

So he called in his master's debtors and asked the first, "How much do you owe?"

"800 gallons of olive oil."

"Take your bill quickly and make it 400."

Then he asked the second, "How much do you owe?"

"1000 bushels of wheat."

"Take your bill and make it 800."

"The master commended the dishonest manager because he acted wisely," Jesus said. "For the people of this world are more clever in dealing with their own kind than are the people of the light. Use worldly wealth to gain friends for yourselves, so that you will be welcomed into eternal dwellings when it's gone.

"Whoever can be trusted with very little can also be trusted with much, and whoever is dishonest with very little will also be dishonest with much. So if you haven't been trustworthy in handling worldly wealth, who will trust you with true riches? And if you haven't been trustworthy with someone else's property, who will give you property of your own?

"No servant can serve two masters. Either he will hate the one and love the other, or he will be devoted to the one and despise the other. You cannot serve both God and money."

The Pharisees heard all this, and they ridiculed Jesus because they loved money.

So Jesus said, "You justify yourselves in the eyes of men but God knows your hearts, and what's highly valued by men is detestable in God's sight. The Law and the Prophets were proclaimed until John. Since that time, the good news of the kingdom of God is being preached and everyone is eager to enter it."

The Coming of the Kingdom of God
LK 17:20-21

The Pharisees asked Jesus when the kingdom of God would come and he replied, "The kingdom of God is not coming in a way that can be observed. People won't say, 'Here it is' or 'There it is,' because the kingdom of God is within you."

The Parable of the Rich Man and Lazarus
LK 16:19-31

A rich man dressed in purple and fine linen lived in luxury every day. At his gate was laid a beggar named Lazarus, covered with sores and longing to eat what fell from the rich man's table. And dogs came and licked his sores.

The beggar died and the angels carried him to Abraham's side. The rich man also died and was buried. In hell, where he was in torment, he looked up and saw Abraham far away, with Lazarus by his side. So he called to him, "Father Abraham, have pity on me and send Lazarus to dip the tip of his finger in water to cool my tongue. I'm in agony in this fire!"

Abraham replied, "Son, remember that in your lifetime you received good things while Lazarus received bad things. But now he's comforted here and you're in agony. However, a great chasm is fixed between us and you. Those who want to cross from here to there are unable to, nor can anyone cross from there to here."

"Then I beg you, send Lazarus to my father's house to warn my five brothers so they can avoid coming to this place of torment."

"They have Moses and the Prophets," Abraham replied. "They should listen to them."

"Father Abraham, I'm sure they'll repent if someone from the dead visits them."

"If they don't listen to Moses and the Prophets, they won't be convinced even if someone rises from the dead."

The Parable of the Unforgiving Servant
MT 18:23-35

The kingdom of heaven is like a king who wanted to settle accounts with his servants. The first man owed him millions of dollars but was unable to pay. So the master ordered that he, his wife, his children, and all that he had be sold to repay the debt.

The servant fell on his knees and begged, "Be patient with me and I'll pay back everything."

So his master took pity on him, canceled the debt, and let him go.

But that servant left and found one of his fellow servants who owed him a few thousand dollars. He grabbed him, choked him, and demanded, "Pay back what you owe me!"

His fellow servant fell to his knees and begged, "Be patient with me and I'll pay you back."

But he refused and put the man in prison until he paid the debt. When the other servants saw what happened, they were very distressed and went and told their master everything.

So the master called the servant in. "You wicked servant," he said, "I canceled all your debt because you begged me to. Shouldn't you have mercy on your fellow servant just as I had on you?" And he was so angry that he turned the servant over to the jailers to be tortured until he paid back everything he owed.

"This is how my heavenly Father will treat each of you unless you forgive your brother from your heart," Jesus concluded.

Jesus Teaches About Forgiveness
MT 18:15-22|LK 17:3-4

Then Jesus said, "If your brother sins against you, show him his fault just between the two of you. If he listens, you've won your brother over. But if he won't listen, take one or two others along so that every dispute may be verified by the testimony of two or three witnesses. If he refuses to listen to them, tell the church, and if he refuses to listen even to the church, treat him as you would a pagan or a tax collector.

"I assure you, whatever you bind on earth will be bound in heaven, and whatever you loose on earth will be loosed in heaven. If two of you on earth agree about anything you ask for, it will be done for you by my Father in heaven. For where two or three come together in my name, I am there among them."

Then Peter asked, "Lord, how many times should I forgive my brother when he sins against me? Up to seven times?"

"Rebuke your brother if he sins and forgive him if he repents," Jesus said. "If he sins against you seven times and returns seven times to ask forgiveness, you must forgive him. But don't stop at seven times, forgive seventy times seven."

Being a Servant
LK 17:7-10

Jesus said, "Suppose your servant is out plowing or caring for the sheep. When he comes in from the field, will you ask him to sit down to eat? No, you are more likely to say, 'Prepare my supper, get yourself ready, and wait on me while I eat and drink, and then you may have your dinner.' So when you've done everything you were told to do, you should say, 'We are unworthy servants and have only done our duty.'"

CHAPTER 10
Teachings and the Raising of Lazarus

Now a man named Lazarus was sick. He and his sisters, Mary and Martha, lived in a village called Bethany.

So the sisters sent a message to Jesus, "Lord, the one you love is sick."

And Jesus said to his disciples, "This sickness won't end in death. No, it's for God's glory, so that his Son may be glorified through it."

Jesus loved Martha, Mary, and Lazarus, yet he stayed where he was two more days. Finally he said to his disciples, "Let's go back to Judea."

"But Rabbi," they said, "you're going back there even though the Jews recently tried to stone you?"

"Aren't there 12 hours of daylight?" Jesus asked. "A man who walks during the day won't stumble, for he sees by this world's light. But he stumbles when he walks at night, because he has no light. Our friend Lazarus has fallen asleep but I'm going to wake him up."

"Lord, if he's asleep he'll get better," his disciples replied, thinking he meant natural sleep.

So Jesus told them plainly, "Lazarus is dead. For your sake I'm glad I wasn't there, so that you may believe. Let's go to him."

Then Thomas said to the rest of the disciples, "Let's go with our Lord so we can die with him."

When Jesus arrived, he found that Lazarus had already been in the tomb four days. Now Bethany was less than two miles from Jerusalem, and many Jews had come to comfort Martha and Mary for the loss of their brother.

Martha heard that Jesus was coming, so she went to meet him, but Mary stayed home.

"Lord," Martha said, "my brother wouldn't have died if you had been here. But even now, I know God will give you whatever you ask."

"Your brother will rise again," Jesus said.

"I know he'll rise again in the resurrection on the last day."

"I am the resurrection and the life. He who believes in me will live even though he dies, and whoever lives and believes in me will never die. Do you believe this?"

"Yes, Lord," Martha said, "I believe you're the Christ, the Son of God, who was to come into the world."

Then Martha returned home and called Mary aside. "The Teacher is here and he's asking for you."

So Mary got up quickly and left.

The Jews who were there comforting her saw her leave. They thought she was going to the tomb to mourn, so they followed her.

Now Jesus hadn't yet entered the village; he was still at the place where Martha had met him. When Mary arrived, she fell at his feet and said, "Lord, my brother wouldn't have died if you had been here."

When Jesus saw her and the Jews who had come with her weeping, he was troubled and deeply moved in his spirit. And Jesus wept with them.

"He really must have loved him!" the Jews said.

But some of them said, "He opened the eyes of the blind man — couldn't he have kept this man from dying?"

Then Jesus asked, "Where did you bury him?"

"Come and see, Lord," they replied.

Jesus was deeply moved as he approached the tomb. It was a cave with a stone laid across the entrance.

"Remove the stone," he said.

"But Lord, he's been there four days," Martha said. "There must be a bad odor by now."

"Like I told you, just believe and you will see the glory of God."

So they took away the stone.

Then Jesus looked up and said, "Father, I thank you that you've heard me. I know you always hear me, but I'm saying this for the benefit of those standing here, so they may believe that you sent me."

Then he shouted, "Lazarus, come out!"

And the dead man came out with his hands and feet wrapped in strips of linen, and a cloth around his face.

"Remove his grave clothes and let him go," Jesus said.

The Jews Plot to Kill Jesus
JN 11:45-54

Now many of the Jews who had come to visit Mary had witnessed Lazarus' resurrection, and they put their faith in Jesus. But some of them went to tell the Pharisees about it.

So the chief priests and the Pharisees called a meeting of the Sanhedrin. "What are we accomplishing?" they asked. "He's performing so many miracles that everyone will believe in him if we let him continue. And then the Romans will take away both our temple and our nation."

Caiaphas the high priest said, "You know nothing at all! Listen, it's better for us to allow one man to die for the people than to allow the whole nation to perish."

He didn't say this on his own. As high priest that year, he prophesied that Jesus would die for the Jewish nation. However, he wouldn't die only for that nation but also for the scattered children of God, to bring them together and make them one.

And from that day on, the Jewish leaders plotted to kill Jesus.

Therefore Jesus no longer traveled publicly among the Jews. Instead he withdrew to a region near the desert, to a village called Ephraim, where he stayed with his disciples.

Jesus Heals Ten Lepers
LK 13:22|LK 17:11-19

Jesus taught throughout the villages and cities as he traveled toward Jerusalem. At the border between Samaria and Galilee, he entered a village and saw ten men who had leprosy.

They stood at a distance and shouted, "Jesus, Master, have pity on us!"

"Go show yourselves to the priests," Jesus said.

And on the way there, they were cleansed.

One of the lepers realized he was healed and returned, praising God in a loud voice. He threw himself at Jesus' feet and thanked him — and he was a Samaritan.

Jesus asked, "Weren't all ten cleansed? Where are the other nine? Did no one else return to give God praise except this foreigner?" Then he said to the man, "Rise and go — your faith has made you well."

Jesus Teaches About Divorce
MT 5:31-32|MT 19:1-12|MK 10:1-12|LK 16:18

Jesus then went into the region of Judea and across the Jordan. Again large crowds closed in on him, and he taught and healed them as he usually did.

Some Pharisees tested him, asking, "Is it lawful for a man to divorce his wife for just any reason?"

"What did Moses command you?" Jesus asked.

"He allowed us to write divorce papers and send the woman away."

"Haven't you read that at the beginning of creation God made them male and female? *For this reason a man must leave his father and mother and unite with his wife, and the two will become one flesh.* So they are no longer two, but one. Therefore, what God joins together no man should separate."

"So why did Moses allow divorce?" they asked.

"Moses wrote the command because your hearts were hard. But from the beginning, that wasn't the intent."

When they returned to the house, the disciples asked Jesus about his statement.

Jesus replied, "It has been said, 'Anyone who divorces his wife must give her a certificate of divorce.' But I assure you that, except for marital unfaithfulness, anyone who divorces his wife and marries another woman commits adultery, and the man who marries a divorced woman commits adultery. And if a woman divorces her husband and marries another man, she commits adultery also."

The disciples said, "In that case it's better not to marry!"

"Not everyone can accept this teaching," Jesus replied. "Indeed, only those to whom God has given understanding can accept it. Some people do choose not to get married: Some were born incapable of sexual activity; others are incapable due to castration; and still others have voluntarily renounced sex and marriage to dedicate themselves to serving God's kingdom."

Jesus Blesses the Children
MT 18:5-7|MT 19:13-15|MK 9:37|MK 9:42
MK 10:13-16|LK 17:1-3|LK 18:15-17

One day little children were brought to Jesus so he could place his hands on them and pray for them. But the disciples rebuked those who brought the children, making Jesus angry.

He called the children to him and said to his disciples, "Allow the children to come to me; don't hinder them, because the kingdom of God belongs to such as these. Whoever welcomes one of these little children in my name welcomes me, and whoever welcomes me welcomes not only me, but the One who sent me.

"Things that cause people to sin will surely occur, but woe to that person through whom they come. It would be better for him to be thrown into the sea with a millstone tied around his neck than to cause one of these little ones to sin, so be careful."

He then took the children in his arms and blessed them, and then he left that place.

Jesus Teaches the Rich Young Man
MT 19:16-30|MK 10:17-31|LK 18:18-30

As Jesus traveled, a ruler ran up to him and fell on his knees. "Good teacher, what must I do to inherit eternal life?" he asked.

"Why do you call me good?" Jesus asked. "No one is good except God alone. But if you want eternal life, obey the commandments."

"Which ones?"

"Don't murder, don't commit adultery, don't steal, don't give false testimony, honor your father and mother, and love your neighbor as yourself."

"Teacher," he declared, "I've obeyed them all since I was a boy. What do I still lack?"

Jesus looked at him with love and said, "If you want to be perfect, sell everything you have and give it to the poor, and you will have treasure in heaven. Then come and follow me."

The young man became unhappy and went away grieving, because he was very wealthy.

Then Jesus said to his disciples, "I assure you, it's hard for a rich man to enter the kingdom of heaven."

And the disciples were amazed by this.

Jesus said again, "Children, how hard it is to enter the kingdom of God! Indeed, it's easier for a camel to go through the eye of a needle than for a rich man to enter the kingdom of God."

The disciples were even more amazed and asked, "Then who can be saved?"

"With man it's impossible, but with God all things are possible."

Peter said, "We've left everything to follow you. What will there be for us?"

Jesus said, "I assure you, when the Son of Man sits on his glorious throne and everything is renewed, you who have followed me will also sit on 12 thrones judging the 12 tribes of Israel. No one who has left wife or children, mother or father, brothers or sisters, or houses or fields for me and the gospel will fail to receive 100 times as much of all these things in this present age — and with them, persecutions — and in the age to come, eternal life. But many who are first will be last, and the last will be first."

The Parable of the Vineyard Workers
MT 20:1-16

The kingdom of heaven is like a landowner who went out early in the morning to hire men to work in his vineyard, agreeing to pay them a normal day's wage.

About 9am he went out again and saw others standing in the marketplace doing nothing. He said, "Go work in my vineyard and I'll pay you whatever is right."

So they went.

He went out again about noon and at 3pm and did the same thing. Around 5pm he went out and found others standing around. He asked them, "Why have you been standing here all day long doing nothing?"

"No one hired us," they said.

"You also go and work in my vineyard."

That evening the owner of the vineyard said to his supervisor, "Call the workers and pay them their wages, beginning with the last ones hired and ending with the first."

The workers who were hired at 5pm each received a full day's wage, so those who were hired first expected to receive more. But each of them received the same pay. They complained to the landowner, "These men who were hired last worked only one hour, but you paid them the same as us, even though we performed most of the work in the heat of the day!"

The landowner said, "Friend, I'm not being unfair to you. Didn't you agree to work for a day's wage? Take your pay and go. I want to give the man who was hired last the same as I gave you. Are you envious because I'm generous? Don't I have the right to do what I want with my own money?"

"So the last will be first, and the first will be last," Jesus concluded.

Jesus Predicts His Death and Resurrection a Third Time
MT 20:17-19|MK 10:32-34|LK 18:31-34

Jesus and his disciples started on their way up to Jerusalem, with Jesus resolutely leading the way. Because of their destination, his disciples were amazed, while others who followed were afraid.

Jesus took the Twelve aside again and said, "Everything written by the prophets about the Son of Man will be fulfilled. He will be betrayed to the chief priests and teachers of the law. They will condemn him to death and hand him over to the Gentiles, who will mock him, spit on him, flog him, and kill him. But on the third day, he will rise again."

The disciples didn't understand any of this because its meaning was hidden from them. They didn't know what he was talking about.

James and John Make a Request
MT 20:20-24|MK 10:35-41

Then James and John approached Jesus, along with their mother, Zebedee's wife, and kneeled down in front of him, Teacher," they said, "we want you to do for us whatever we ask."

"What is it you want?" he asked.

Their mother replied, "In your kingdom, please allow one of my two sons to sit at your right and the other at your left."

"You don't know what you're asking," Jesus said to James and John. "Can you drink the cup I drink or be baptized with the baptism I'm baptized with?"

"We can," they said.

"Indeed you *will* drink the cup I drink and be baptized with the baptism I'm baptized with, but to sit at my right or left isn't for me to grant. These places belong to those for whom my Father prepared them."

When the other ten disciples heard about this, they were angry with James and John.

The Disciples Argue About Who's the Greatest
MT 18:1-4|MT 20:25-28|MK 9:33b-36
MK 10:42-45|LK 9:46-48|LK 22:24-30

Later the disciples asked Jesus, "Who is the greatest in the kingdom of heaven?"

"What were you arguing about on the road?" Jesus asked.

But they remained quiet because that's what they had been arguing about.

Jesus knew their thoughts, so he called them together and said, "You know that those who are regarded as rulers of the Gentiles lord it over them, and their high officials exercise authority over them. But it shouldn't be that way with you. Instead, anyone wants to be first must be the very last, and the slave of all.

"The greatest among you should be like the youngest, and the one who rules like the one who serves. Who is greater, the one at the table or the one who serves? Isn't it the one at the table? But even the Son of Man didn't come to be served, but to serve, and to give his life as a ransom for many.

"You have stood by me in my trials, and I confer on you a kingdom just as my Father conferred one on me. Then you will eat and drink at my table in my kingdom and sit on thrones, judging the twelve tribes of Israel."

He took a little child and had him stand among them. Then he held him in his arms and said, "I assure you, unless you change and become like little children, you will never enter the kingdom of heaven. Therefore whoever humbles himself like this child is the greatest in the kingdom of heaven.

Jesus Restores Blind Bartimaeus' Sight
MT 20:29-34|MK 10:46-52|LK 18:35-43

As Jesus and his disciples approached Jericho, with a large crowd following, two blind men sat begging by the roadside.

One of them was Bartimaeus (Son of Timaeus). When he heard the crowd going by, he asked what was happening. They told him, "Jesus of Nazareth is passing by."

So Bartimaeus and the other man shouted, "Lord, Son of David, have mercy on us!"

Many people in the front told them to be quiet, but the men shouted even louder, "Lord, Son of David, have mercy on us!"

Jesus stopped and said, "Call them."

So they said to the blind men, "He's calling you. Cheer up and come on over."

Bartimaeus threw his coat aside, jumped to his feet, and came to Jesus, along with the other man.

"What do you want me to do for you?" Jesus asked.

"Lord, we want to see."

Jesus had compassion on them and touched their eyes. "Receive your sight. Your faith has healed you."

Immediately they could see and they followed Jesus, praising God. Those who witnessed the healing also praised God.

Zacchaeus the Tax Collector Repents
LK 19:1-10

Jesus then passed through Jericho, where Zacchaeus, a wealthy chief tax collector lived. Jesus was coming his way, but Zacchaeus was too short and couldn't see because the crowd was blocking his view. So Zacchaeus ran ahead and climbed a sycamore-fig tree so he could see Jesus.

When Jesus reached that spot, he looked up and said, "Zacchaeus, come down immediately. I must stay at your house today."

So he came down and welcomed Jesus gladly.

The people complained, "He's gone to be the guest of a sinner!"

But Zacchaeus stood up and said, "Look, Lord! Here and now I give half of my possessions to the poor, and if I've cheated anybody, I'll pay back four times the amount."

Jesus said, "Today salvation has come to this house, for this man is a true son of Abraham. The Son of Man came to seek and to save what was lost."

The Parable of the Ten Minas
LK 19:11-28

Then Jesus told them a parable because he was near Jerusalem and the people thought that the kingdom of God was going to appear immediately:

> A man of noble birth went to a distant country to have himself appointed king, planning to return. So he called ten of his servants and gave them ten minas. "Put this money to work until I come back," he said.
>
> But his subjects hated him and sent a delegation after him with a message, "We don't want this man to be our king."
>
> Nevertheless, he was made king and he returned home. Then he sent for the servants to find out what they had gained with the money he'd given them.
>
> The first one said, "Sir, your mina earned ten more."
>
> "Well done, my good servant!" his master replied. "Take charge of ten cities because you've been trustworthy in a very small matter."
>
> The second servant said, "Sir, your mina earned five more."
>
> "Take charge of five cities."
>
> Another servant said, "Sir, here is your mina; I kept it safe in a piece of cloth. I was afraid of you because you're a harsh man. You take profits you haven't worked for and you harvest grain you haven't planted."
>
> "I'll judge you by your own words, you wicked servant! So you knew that I'm a hard man, taking out what I didn't put

in and harvesting what I didn't plant? Then why didn't you deposit my money so I could collect it with interest when I returned?" Then he said to those standing by, "Take his mina away and give it to the one who has ten."

"Sir," they said, "he already has ten!"

"I assure you, to everyone who has, more will be given, but for the one who has nothing, even what he has will be taken away. Now bring me those enemies who didn't want me to be their king and kill them in front of me."

Then Jesus continued on to Jerusalem.

The Jews Travel to Jerusalem for Passover
JN 11:55-57|JN 12:9-11

When it was almost time for the Passover, many traveled from the country to Jerusalem for their ceremonial cleansing.

They stood in the temple area and kept looking for Jesus, asking each other, "Do you think he's coming to the Feast at all?"

The chief priests and Pharisees had ordered that anyone who knew where Jesus was should report it so they could arrest him.

PART V
JESUS' FINAL WEEK

CHAPTER 11
Saturday, Sunday, & Monday

SATURDAY

Mary Anoints Jesus at Bethany
MT 26:6-13|MK 14:3-9|JN 11:2|JN 12:1-8

Six days before the Passover, Jesus arrived at Simon the Leper's house in Bethany, where a dinner was given in his honor. Martha served and Lazarus was among those reclining at the table with him.

Then their sister Mary brought in an alabaster jar of very expensive perfume made of pure nard. She broke the jar and poured the perfume on Jesus' head. She also poured it on his feet and wiped them with her hair, filling the house with the perfume's fragrance.

Judas Iscariot, the disciple who would later betray Jesus, objected and rebuked her harshly, "Why this waste of perfume? It could have been sold for more than a year's wages and the money given to the poor."

He didn't say this because he cared about the poor but because he was a thief. He was responsible for the money bag and he frequently helped himself to its contents.

"Why are you bothering her? Leave her alone," Jesus said. "She's done a beautiful thing for me. You will always have the poor with you and can help them anytime you want. But you won't always have me. She did what she could, pouring this perfume on my body to prepare me for burial. I assure you, what she has done will be told wherever the gospel is preached throughout the world, in memory of her."

A large crowd of Jews found out he was there and went not only to see him but also to see Lazarus, whom Jesus had raised from the dead.

So the chief priests made plans to kill Lazarus too, because he was the reason many Jews were deserting them and believing in Jesus.

SUNDAY

The Crowd Welcomes Jesus to Jerusalem
MT 21:1-11|MT 21:14-17|MK 11:1-11|MK 11:19
LK 13:34-35|LK 19:29-44|JN 12:12-19

The next day as they approached Jerusalem, they arrived at the hill called the Mount of Olives, near Bethphage and Bethany.

Jesus told two of his disciples, "Go to the village just ahead. As you enter it, you will find a donkey tied there with her colt, which no one has ever ridden. Untie them and bring them to me. If anyone asks why, tell him, 'The Lord needs them and will send them back shortly.'"

This fulfilled what was spoken through the prophet: *Say to the Daughter of Zion, "See, your king comes to you, gentle and riding on a donkey — on a colt, the foal of a donkey."*

So the disciples went and found the animals in the street, tied at a doorway, and they untied them.

"Why are you taking them?" the owners asked.

"The Lord needs them."

So the owners let them go.

The disciples brought the animals to Jesus and threw their robes over the colt, and he sat on it.

The next day the huge crowd that came for the Feast heard that Jesus was on his way to Jerusalem. As he approached the place where the road descends from the Mount of Olives, his followers took palm branches they had cut from trees in the fields and went to meet him. They spread their robes on the road as he passed by and joyfully praised God in loud voices for all the miracles they had seen.

The crowds ahead of him and behind him shouted, "Hosanna to the Son of David! Blessed is the King of Israel who comes in the name of the Lord! Peace in heaven and glory in the highest heaven!"

Some of the Pharisees said to Jesus, "Teacher, rebuke your disciples!"

"I assure you," he replied, "even if they remain quiet, the stones will cry out."

As Jesus approached Jerusalem, he wept over the city and said, "Jerusalem, Jerusalem, you kill the prophets and stone those sent to you. I've often longed to gather your children together as a hen gathers her chicks under her wings, but you weren't willing! If only you had known today what would bring you peace, but now it's hidden from you. Look, your house is forsaken! The time is coming when your enemies will set up a barricade to surround you and hem you in on every side. They will crush you to the ground, you and the children with you. They won't leave one stone upon another, because you didn't recognize the time of God's coming to you. Most assuredly, you won't see me again until you say, 'Blessed is he who comes in the name of the Lord.'"

His disciples didn't immediately understand all of this. It was only after Jesus was glorified that they realized what had been written about him was being fulfilled.

When Jesus entered Jerusalem, the whole city was excited and asked, "Who is he?"

"It's Jesus," the crowds kept answering, "the prophet from Nazareth in Galilee."

Now the same crowd was there that was present when Jesus had raised Lazarus from the dead and called him from the tomb. And they continued to spread the word about what had happened. Therefore many people who heard about the miracle went to see him.

"This is getting us nowhere," the Pharisees said to each other. "Look how the whole world is following after him!"

When Jesus entered Jerusalem, he went to the temple. The blind and the lame came to him and he healed them. But the chief priests and the teachers of the law were indignant when they saw the wonderful things he did and heard the children in the temple area shouting, "Hosanna to the Son of David."

"Do you hear what these children are saying?" they asked.

"Yes," Jesus replied. "Clearly you've never read, *From the lips of children and infants, you have ordained praise.*"

It was getting late, so after Jesus looked around at everything in the temple, he left the city and went to Bethany. Each evening he and the Twelve spent the night there, as was their habit.

MONDAY
Jesus Curses a Fig Tree and Clears the Temple
MT 21:12-13|MT 21:18-19|MK 11:12-18|LK 19:45-46

Early the next morning, when they left Bethany to return to Jerusalem, Jesus saw a fig tree in the distance. He was hungry so he went to see if it had any fruit. However, he found only leaves, because it wasn't the season for figs.

His disciples heard him say to the tree, "May no one ever eat fruit from you again!"

And the tree died immediately.

When Jesus reached Jerusalem, he entered the temple area and threw out those who were buying and selling there. He overturned the tables of the money changers and the benches of those selling doves, and wouldn't allow anyone to carry merchandise through the temple courts.

He said, "It is written, *My house will be called a house of prayer for all nations, but you've turned it into a den of thieves.*"

When the chief priests and teachers of the law heard this, they began looking for a way to kill him. They were afraid of him because the crowd was astonished by his teachings.

Jesus Predicts His Crucifixion
LK 19:47-48|JN 12:20-50

Some Greeks were there to worship at the Feast. They went to Philip, who was from Bethsaida in Galilee, and said, "Sir, we'd like to see Jesus."

Philip told Andrew and they both went to tell Jesus.

Jesus replied, "The hour has come for the Son of Man to be glorified. I assure you, unless a kernel of wheat falls to the ground and dies, it remains only a single seed. But if it dies it produces many seeds. Whoever loves his life will lose it, but whoever hates his life in this world will keep it for eternity. Whoever serves me must follow me, and where I am, my servant will be also. My Father will honor the one who serves me.

"Now my heart is troubled but will I ask the Father to save me from this hour? No, it was for this very reason that I came. Father, glorify your name!"

Then a voice from heaven said, "I have glorified it and will glorify it again."

The crowd heard it and said it was thunder; others said an angel had spoken.

Jesus said, "This voice was for your benefit, not mine. Now is the time for judgment on this world; now the prince of this world will be driven out. But when I am lifted up from the earth, I will draw everyone to me."

He said this to demonstrate how he was going to die.

The crowd said, "The Law says that the Christ will remain forever, so how can you say the Son of Man must be lifted up? Who is this 'Son of Man'?"

"You are going to have the light just a little while longer," Jesus said. "Walk while you have the light, before darkness overtakes you. He who walks in the dark doesn't know where he's going. Put your trust in the light while you have it, so that you may become sons of the light."

Even after Jesus performed many miracles in their presence, they still wouldn't believe in him. This fulfilled the word of Isaiah the prophet:

Lord, who has believed our message and to who has the arm of the Lord been revealed?

They simply couldn't believe because, as Isaiah says elsewhere: *He blinded their eyes and deadened their hearts, so they can neither see with their eyes nor understand with their hearts, nor turn and allow me to heal them.* Isaiah was speaking about Jesus because he saw his glory.

Yet many did believe in Jesus, even among the leaders. But they wouldn't confess their faith because of the Pharisees, fearing they would be put out of the synagogue. They loved praise from men more than praise from God.

Then Jesus cried out, "When a man believes in me, he doesn't believe in me only, but in the One who sent me. When he looks at me, he sees the One who sent me. I've come into the world as a light, so that no one who believes in me should stay in darkness.

"But I don't judge the person who hears my words and doesn't keep them. I didn't come to judge the world, but to save it. There is a judge for the one who rejects me and doesn't accept my words; that very word I spoke will condemn him at the last day. I didn't speak of my own accord, but the Father who sent me told me what to say and how to say it. I know his command leads to eternal life, so whatever I say is just what the Father told me to say."

The chief priests and the teachers of the law heard about this and began looking for a way to kill Jesus, because they were afraid of him. But they couldn't find a way even though he taught in the temple every day, because the crowd was amazed at his teaching and they hung on his words.

That evening Jesus hid himself from them. He left the city and spent the night in Bethany.

CHAPTER 12
Tuesday

The Lesson of the Withered Fig Tree
MT 21:20-22|MK 11:20-24

In the morning the disciples saw that the fig tree had dried up from the roots. Peter remembered what happened the day before and said, "Rabbi, look! The fig tree you cursed is dead!"

The disciples were amazed. "How did it die so quickly?" they asked.

"Have faith in God," Jesus said. "I assure you, anyone who has faith and doesn't doubt in his heart can do the same. Not only can you do what was done to the fig tree, but anyone can say to this mountain, 'Throw yourself into the sea.' Believe you have received whatever you ask for in prayer, and it will be yours."

The Jewish Leaders Challenge Jesus' Authority
MT 21:23-27|MK 11:27-33|LK 20:1-8

They arrived in Jerusalem. As Jesus taught in the temple courts and preached the gospel, the chief priests, teachers of the law, and the elders approached him and asked, "Who gave you the authority to do these things?"

Jesus said, "I'll tell you if you answer my question: Where did John's baptism come from? From heaven or from men? Tell me."

They discussed it among themselves and said, "If we say 'From heaven,' he'll ask why we didn't believe John. But if we say 'From men,' all the people will stone us because they're persuaded that John was a genuine prophet."

So they said to Jesus, "We don't know where it came from."

"Neither will I tell you by what authority I'm doing these things," Jesus said.

The Parable of the Two Sons
MT 21:28-32

Jesus continued:

A man had two sons. He said to the first, "Son, go work in the vineyard today."

"No," he said, but later he changed his mind and went.

Then the father asked the other son the same thing. He said, "I will, sir," but he didn't go.

"What do you think? Which of the two did what his father wanted?" Jesus asked.

The first," the Jewish leaders said.

"I assure you, the tax collectors and the prostitutes are entering the kingdom of God ahead of you. John came to show you the way of righteousness. You didn't believe him, but the tax collectors and the prostitutes did. And even after you witnessed this, you didn't believe him and repent."

The Parable of the Greedy Vineyard Farmers
MT 21:33-44|MK 12:1-11|LK 20:9-18

Jesus told another parable:

A landowner planted a vineyard. He put a wall around it, dug a pit for the winepress, and built a watchtower. Then he rented the vineyard to some farmers and went away on a long journey.

At harvest time he sent a servant to gather some grapes from the vineyard. But the farmers seized him, beat him, and sent him away empty-handed. Then the landowner sent another servant; they hit him on the head and treated him shamefully. He sent still another, and they killed him.

He sent more servants than the first time, and the farmers treated them the same way.

He had one left to send, a son he loved. "Maybe they'll respect my son," he said.

But the farmers said to one another, "This is the heir; let's kill him and take his inheritance."

So they killed him and threw him out of the vineyard.

"Therefore," Jesus said, "when the owner of the vineyard returns, what will he do to those farmers? He will bring those wretches to a wretched end and rent the vineyard to others, who will give him his share of the crop at harvest time."

"May this never be!" the people replied.

Jesus said, "Have you never read in the Scriptures: *The stone the builders rejected became the cornerstone; this came from the Lord and it is marvelous in our eyes.*

"Therefore I assure you, the kingdom of God will be taken away from you and given to a nation that will produce its fruit. He who falls on this stone will be broken to pieces, but he on whom it falls will be crushed."

The Parable of the Wedding Banquet
MT 22:1-14

Jesus spoke in parables again, saying:

> The kingdom of heaven is like a king who prepared a wedding banquet for his son. He sent his servants to get those who had been invited, but they refused to come.
>
> He sent more servants and said, "Tell them to come to the wedding banquet. My oxen and fattened cattle have been butchered. I've prepared dinner and everything is ready."
>
> But they paid no attention and went off — one to his field, another to his business. The rest seized his servants, mistreated them, and killed them. The king was enraged. He sent his army to destroy those murderers and burn their city.
>
> Then he said to his servants, "The wedding banquet is ready, but those I invited didn't deserve to come. Go to the street corners and invite anyone you find."
>
> So the servants gathered all the people they could find, both good and bad, and the wedding hall was filled with guests.
>
> But the king noticed a man among the guests who wasn't wearing wedding clothes.
>
> "Friend," he asked, "how did you get in here without wedding clothes?"
>
> The man was speechless.
>
> Then the king told the attendants, "Tie him hand and foot and throw him outside into the darkness, where there will be weeping and gnashing of teeth."

"For many are invited, but few are chosen," Jesus concluded.

Jesus Rebukes the Scribes and Pharisees
MT 23:1-24|MT 23:29-36|MK 12:38-40
LK 11:42-43|LK 11:45|LK 11:47-52|LK 20:45-47

Then Jesus said to the crowds and to his disciples, "The teachers of the law and the Pharisees sit in Moses' seat, so you must obey them and do everything they tell you. But don't do what they do, because they don't practice what they preach. Everything they do is just to show off for others. They like to walk around in flowing robes. They make extra-wide scripture bands for their arms and forehead, and long tassels for their clothes. They love the place of honor at banquets and the most important seats in the synagogues.

"They love to be greeted in the marketplaces and have others call them 'Rabbi.' But don't allow anyone to call you 'Rabbi,' because you have only one Master and you're all brothers. And don't call anyone on earth 'father,' because you have one Father and he is in heaven. Nor should you let anyone call you 'teacher,' because you have one Teacher, the Christ. The greatest among you will be your servant. For whoever exalts himself will be humbled, and whoever humbles himself will be exalted."

Then he said, "Woe to you Pharisees, you hypocrites! You shut the kingdom of heaven in men's faces. You yourselves don't enter, but you're preventing others who want to enter. You travel over land and sea to win a single convert, and when he converts you make him twice as much a son of hell as you are.

"Woe to you, blind guides! You say swearing by the temple means nothing, but anyone who swears by the gold of the temple is bound by his oath. You blind fools! Which is greater: the gold or the temple that makes the gold sacred? You also say swearing by the altar means nothing, but anyone who swears by the gift on the altar is bound by his oath. You blind men! Which is greater: the gift or the altar that makes the gift sacred? Therefore, he who swears by the altar swears by it and by everything on it. And he who swears by the temple swears by it and by the one who dwells in it. And he who swears by heaven swears by God's throne and by the one who sits on it.

"Woe to you Pharisees, you hypocrites! You give a tenth of your spices — mint, dill, and cummin — but you've ignored the more important matters of the law: justice, mercy, and faithfulness. You should have practiced the latter without neglecting the former. You blind guides! You strain out a gnat but swallow a camel.

One of the experts in the law said, "Teacher, you insult us too when you say these things."

Jesus replied, "And woe to you experts in the law! You load people down with burdens they can hardly carry, and you won't lift one finger to help them. You devour widows' houses and make lengthy prayers to show off. Such men will be punished severely.

"Woe to you experts in the law; you've taken away the key to knowledge. You yourselves haven't entered, and you've hindered those who were entering.

"Woe to you; your forefathers killed the prophets and you built their tombs. In this way you show approval of what they did. Therefore God in his wisdom said, 'I'll send them prophets and apostles, some of whom they will kill and others they will persecute.' Therefore this generation will be held responsible for the bloodshed of all the prophets since the beginning of the world, from the blood of Abel to the blood of Zechariah, who was killed between the altar and the sanctuary. Yes, I assure you, this generation will be held responsible for it all!"

The Jewish Leaders Ask About Paying Taxes to Caesar
MT 21:45-46|MT 22:15-22|MK 12:12-17
LK 11:53-54|LK 20:19-26

The chief priests and the Pharisees knew Jesus' parables were about them. They looked for a way to arrest him immediately, but they were afraid of the crowd because the people considered him a prophet. After they parted ways, the Pharisees and the teachers of the law became very hostile toward Jesus and they kept a close eye on him, waiting for the opportunity to provoke him with countless questions. They sent some Pharisees and Herodians who pretended to be righteous, hoping to trap him so they could hand him over to the power and authority of the governor.

"Teacher," they said, "you're a man of integrity. We know you speak and teach what is right. You don't show partiality but teach the way of God in accordance with the truth. In your opinion, is it lawful to pay taxes to Caesar? Should we pay or not?"

Jesus knew their motives were evil, so he said, "You hypocrites, why are you testing me? Show me the coin used to pay the tax."

So they brought him a denarius.

"Whose image and inscription is on this coin?" he asked.

"Caesar's," they replied.

"Then give to Caesar what belongs to Caesar, and give to God what belongs to God."

And they were amazed by his answer. Since they were unable to trap him, they became silent and left him.

The Sadducees Ask About Resurrection and Marriage
MT 22:23-33|MK 12:18-27|LK 20:27-39

That same day some Sadducees, who say there is no resurrection, approached Jesus. "Teacher," they said, "Moses wrote that if a man's brother dies and leaves a wife but no children, he must marry the widow and have children for his brother.

"Now there were seven brothers among us. The first one married and died. He had no children, so he left his wife to his brother. The second one married the widow but he also died, leaving no child. It was the same with the third. In the same way all seven died, leaving no children. Finally, the woman died too. Now whose wife will she be at the resurrection, since all seven were married to her?"

"You are mistaken because you don't know the Scriptures or the power of God," Jesus said. "The people of this age marry and are given in marriage. But those who are considered worthy of taking part in that age and in the resurrection from the dead will neither marry nor be given in marriage. They are like the angels, so they can no longer die. And they are God's children because they are children of the resurrection.

"Now about the dead rising, haven't you read the account of the bush in the book of Moses? God said, *I am the God of Abraham, the God of Isaac, and the God of Jacob.* He isn't the God of the dead, but of the living, for to him all are alive. You are badly mistaken!"

The crowds were amazed at his teaching, and some teachers of the law responded, "Well said, teacher!"

A Pharisee Asks About the Greatest Commandment
MT 22:34-40|MK 12:28-34a

The Pharisees heard that Jesus had given a good answer and silenced the Sadducees. So they gathered together and sent an expert in the law to test him too. "Which is the most important of all the commandments?" he asked Jesus.

"The most important one is this: *Hear, O Israel, the Lord our God, the Lord is one. Love the Lord your God with all your heart, with all your soul, with all your mind, and with all your strength.* The second is this: *Love your neighbor as yourself.* All the Law and the Prophets is based on these two commandments, and no commandment is greater."

"Well said, teacher," the man replied. "You're right! God is one and there's no other but him. To love him with all your heart, all your understanding, and all your strength, and to love your neighbor as yourself, is more important than all burnt offerings and sacrifices."

Since he had responded wisely, Jesus said, "You are not far from the kingdom of God."

Whose Son Is the Christ?
MT 22:41-46|MK 12:34b-37|LK 20:40-44

While Jesus was teaching in the temple courts, the Pharisees gathered together there. Jesus asked them, "What do you think about the Christ? Whose son is he?"

"The son of David," they replied.

"So how can David, speaking by the Spirit, call him 'Lord'? For he himself declares in the book of Psalms, *The Lord said to my Lord: 'Sit at my right hand until I make your enemies your footstool.'* Since David calls him 'Lord,' how can he be his son?"

The large crowd listened to him with delight, and no one could say a word in reply. From then on, no one dared ask him any more questions.

The Parable of the Pharisee and the Tax Collector
LK 18:9-14

To some who were confident of their own righteousness and looked down on everybody else, Jesus told this parable:

> Two men went to pray in the temple, one a Pharisee and the other a tax collector. The Pharisee stood up and prayed, "God, I thank you that I'm not like other men — robbers, evildoers, adulterers — or even like this tax collector. I fast twice a week and give a tenth of everything."
>
> But the tax collector stood at a distance. He wouldn't even look up to heaven but beat his chest and said, "God, have mercy on me, a sinner."

"I assure you that only the tax collector went home justified before God," Jesus said. "For everyone who exalts himself will be humbled and he who humbles himself will be exalted."

A Widow Gives a Sacrificial Offering
MK 12:41-44|LK 21:1-4

Jesus sat across from the temple treasury and watched the crowd give their offering. Many rich people threw in large amounts, but a poor widow put in two very small copper coins, worth only a fraction of a penny.

Jesus said to his disciples, "I assure you, this poor widow put more into the treasury than everyone else. They all gave out of their wealth, but she gave out of her poverty and put in everything — all she had to live on."

Now the temple was adorned with beautiful stones and gifts dedicated to God. As they were leaving the temple, one of Jesus' disciples said, "Look, Teacher! What massive stones! What magnificent buildings!"

"The time will come when all of this will be destroyed," Jesus replied. "Not one stone will be left upon another — every one of them will be thrown down."

As he sat on the Mount of Olives across from the temple, Peter, James, John, and Andrew asked him privately, "When will these things happen, and what will be the sign that they're about to be fulfilled? What will be the sign of your coming and the end of the age?"

Jesus replied, "The time is coming when you will long to see one of the days of the Son of Man, but you won't see it. Don't be afraid when you hear of wars and revolutions. These things must happen first, but the end won't come right away. Nation will rise against nation, and kingdom against kingdom. Great earthquakes, famines, and deadly diseases will occur in various places, along with fearful events and great signs from heaven. All these are the beginning of birth pains.

"You must be on your guard. Before all these things take place, they will lay hands on you and persecute you. You will be handed over to the local councils and flogged in the synagogues. Because of me, you will stand before governors and kings as witnesses to them. But whenever you're arrested and brought to trial, decide beforehand not to worry about how you will defend yourselves. Just say whatever is given to you at the time, because it isn't you speaking but the Holy Spirit. I will give you words and wisdom that none of your adversaries will be able to resist or contradict.

"Many will turn away from the faith and betray and hate each other. Even parents, brothers, relatives, and friends will betray you, and some of you will be killed. False prophets will appear and deceive many people. Because of the increase of wickedness, the love of most will grow cold. All men will hate you because of me, but not a hair of your head will perish. He who stands firm to the end will be saved. And this gospel of the kingdom will be preached throughout the whole world as a testimony to all nations, and then the end will come.

"When you see Jerusalem surrounded by armies, you will know that its desolation (spoken of through the prophet Daniel — let the reader understand) is near. Then those in Judea should flee to the mountains, those in the city should get out, and those in the country should not enter the city. No one on his rooftop should go down to get anything from the house. And no one in the field should go back to get his coat. For this is the time of punishment in fulfillment of everything that has been written.

"It will be dreadful in those days for pregnant women and nursing mothers! There will be great distress in the land and wrath against this nation. They will fall by the sword and be taken as prisoners to all the nations. Jerusalem will be trampled on by the Gentiles until the times of the Gentiles are fulfilled.

"Pray that your flight won't take place in winter or on the Sabbath. For then there will be great distress, unequaled from the beginning of the world until now. No one would survive if the Lord hadn't cut short those days, but he shortened them for the sake of the elect, whom he chose.

"Immediately after those distressing days: *The sun will be darkened and the moon won't give its light; the stars will fall from the sky and the heavenly bodies will be shaken.*

On earth, nations will be in anguish and confusion at the roaring and tossing of the sea. Men will faint from terror, apprehensive of what is coming upon the world. Make sure you aren't deceived, for many will come in my name claiming, *'I am the Christ'* and *'The time is near.'* They will deceive many, but don't follow them. If anyone says, *'Look, here is the Christ!'* or *'Look, there he is!'* don't believe it. If they say, *'There he is out in the desert,'* don't go out. Or, *'Here he is in the inner rooms,'* don't believe it. False Christs and false prophets will appear and perform signs and miracles to deceive the elect — if that were possible. So be on your guard; I'm telling you everything ahead of time. I assure you, this generation will certainly not pass away until all these things have occurred. Heaven and earth will pass away, but my words will never pass away.

"Now just as lightning that comes from the east is visible even in the west, so will be the coming of the Son of Man. But first he must suffer many things and be rejected by this generation.

"At that time the sign of the Son of Man will appear in the sky, and all the nations of the earth will mourn. They will see him coming on the clouds of the sky, with power and great glory. When these things begin to take place, stand up and lift up your heads, because your redemption is drawing near. He will send his angels with a loud trumpet call, and they will gather his elect from the four winds, from the ends of the earth to the ends of the heavens.

"Now learn this lesson from the fig tree: As soon as its twigs get tender and its leaves come out, you know that summer is near. In the same way when you see these things happening, you know that the kingdom of God is near, right at the door."

Jesus Came to Cause Division
MT 10:34-36|LK 12:49-53

"I've come to bring fire upon the earth, and how I wish it were already kindled! But I have a baptism to undergo, and how distressed I am until it's completed! Do you think I came to bring peace on earth? No, I came to bring a sword, and division. From now on there will be five in one family divided against each other, three against two and two against three. I've come to turn *a man against his father, a daughter against her mother, a daughter-in-law against her mother-in-law. A man's enemies will be the members of his own household.*"

The Sheep and the Goats
MT 25:31-46|LK 21:34-35

"When the Son of Man comes in his glory with all the angels, he will sit on his throne in heavenly glory. All the nations will be gathered before him, and he will separate the people one from another, as a shepherd separates the sheep from the goats. He will put the sheep on his right and the goats on his left.

"Then the King will say to those on his right, 'Come, you who are blessed by my Father; take your inheritance, the kingdom prepared for you since the creation of the world. For I was hungry and you gave me something to eat, I was thirsty and you gave me something to drink, I was a stranger and you invited me in, I needed clothes and you clothed me, I was sick and you looked after me, I was in prison and you came to visit me.'

"Then the righteous will say, 'Lord, when did we see you hungry and feed you, or thirsty and give you something to drink? When did we see you a stranger and invite you in, or needing clothes and clothe you? When did we see you sick or in prison and go visit you?'

"The King will reply, 'I assure you, whatever you did for the least of these brothers of mine, you did for me.'

"Then he will say to those on his left, 'Depart from me, you who are cursed, into the eternal fire prepared for the devil and his angels. For I was hungry and you gave me nothing to eat, I was thirsty and you gave me nothing to drink, I was a stranger and you didn't invite me in, I needed clothes and you didn't clothe me, I was sick and in prison and you didn't look after me.'

"They also will answer, 'Lord, when did we see you hungry or thirsty or a stranger or needing clothes or sick or in prison and didn't help you?'

"He will reply, 'I assure you, whatever you failed to do for the least of these, you failed to do for me.'

"Then they will go away to eternal punishment, but the righteous to eternal life.

"Be careful. Don't allow yourselves to be weighed down with overindulgence, drunkenness, and the worries of life. Otherwise, that day will come upon you unexpectedly like a trap, for it will come upon all those who live upon the face of the whole earth."

The Parable of the Wise and Foolish Virgins
MT 25:1-13

At that time the kingdom of heaven will be like ten virgins who went to meet the bridegroom. The five foolish women took their lamps but didn't take any oil. But the five wise women took oil in jars along with their lamps. The bridegroom took a long time to arrive, and they all became drowsy and fell asleep.

At midnight someone cried out, "The bridegroom is here! Come out to meet him!"

So the virgins woke up and trimmed their lamps. The foolish women said to the wise, "Give us some of your oil — our lamps are going out."

"No," they replied, "there may not be enough for both us and you. Go buy some from those who sell oil."

But the bridegroom arrived while they were on their way to buy the oil. The virgins who were ready went in with him to the wedding banquet. And the door was shut.

Later the others also returned. "Sir! Sir!" they said. "Open the door for us!"

But he replied, "I assure you, I don't know you."

"So be alert, because you don't know the day or the hour," Jesus concluded.

The Parable of the Talents
MT 25:14-30

Again, it will be like a man going on a journey who entrusted his money to his servants. To one he gave five talents, to another two talents, and to another one talent, each according to his ability. Then he went on his journey.

The man who received five talents immediately put his money to work and gained five more. The one with the two talents gained two more. But the man who received one talent dug a hole in the ground and hid his master's money.

After a long time, the master returned and settled accounts with them. The first man said, "Master, you entrusted me with five talents — look, I've gained five more."

His master replied, "Well done, good and faithful servant! You've been faithful with a few things; I'll put you in charge of many things. Come and share your master's happiness!"

The second man said, "Master, you entrusted me with two talents — look, I've gained two more."

"Well done, good and faithful servant! You've been faithful with a few things; I'll put you in charge of many things. Come and share your master's happiness!"

Then the last man said, "Master, I know you're a harsh man, harvesting where you haven't planted and gathering where you haven't scattered seed. So I was afraid and hid your talent in the ground. Look, here is what belongs to you."

His master replied, "You wicked, lazy servant! So you knew that I harvest where I haven't planted and gather where I haven't scattered seed? Then you should have deposited my money with the bankers so I could have received it back with interest when I returned.

"Take the talent from him and give it to the one who has ten talents. For everyone who has will be given more, and he will have an abundance. Whoever doesn't have, even what he has will be taken from him. Now throw that worthless servant outside into the darkness, where there will be weeping and gnashing of teeth."

"No one knows the day or hour the Son of Man will come, not even the angels in heaven or the Son. Only the Father knows. As it was in the days of Noah, so it will be at the coming of the Son of Man. For in the days before the flood, up to the day Noah entered the ark, people were eating and drinking, marrying and giving in marriage. They knew nothing about what would happen until the flood came and washed them all away. That's how it will be when the Son of Man comes.

"It was the same in the days of Lot. People were eating and drinking, buying and selling, planting and building. But on the day Lot left Sodom, fire and sulfur rained down from heaven and destroyed them all. That's how it will be when the Son of Man comes.

"Remember Lot's wife! Whoever tries to keep his life will lose it, and whoever loses his life will preserve it. I assure you, on that night two people will be in one bed: one will be taken and the other left. Two men will be in the field: one will be taken and the other left. Two women will be grinding with a hand mill: one will be taken and the other left."

"Where, Lord?" they asked.

"Where there is a dead body, vultures will gather," Jesus replied.

"Therefore keep watch, because you don't know on what day your Lord will come. But understand this: If the owner of the house had known what time of night the thief was coming, he would have kept watch and not let his house be broken into. You must also be ready, because the Son of Man will come at an hour you don't expect him.

"Be dressed and ready for service and keep your lamps burning, like men waiting for their master to return from a wedding banquet, so that when he knocks they can immediately open the door for him. It will be good for those servants whose master finds them watching when he comes. It will be good for those servants whose master finds them ready, even if he comes in the second or third watch of the night. I assure you, he will dress himself to serve, have them recline at the table, and wait on them.

"Who then is the faithful and wise servant, whom the master puts in charge to manage his servants and give them their food allowance at the proper time? It will be good for that servant if the master finds him doing his work when he returns. I assure you, he will put him in charge of all his possessions. But suppose the servant says to himself, *My master is taking a long time to return*, and he beats the male and female servants and eats, drinks, and gets drunk. His master will return on a day he doesn't expect and at an hour in which he is unaware. He will cut that servant to pieces and assign him a place with the unbelievers, where there will be weeping and gnashing of teeth.

"That servant who knows his master's will and doesn't do it will be beaten with many blows. But the one who doesn't know and does things deserving punishment will be beaten with few blows. From everyone who has been given much, much will be demanded. And from the one who has been entrusted with much, much more will be asked.

"Be on guard! Be alert! You don't know when that time will come. It's like a man who leaves his house and puts his servants in charge, each with his assigned task, and tells the one at the door to keep watch.

"So keep watch, because you don't know when the owner of the house will return — whether in the evening, at midnight, when the rooster crows, or at dawn. If he comes suddenly, don't let him find you sleeping. What I say to you, I say to everyone — Watch! And pray that you are able to escape all that's about to happen, and that you may be able to stand before the Son of Man."

Each evening Jesus spent the night on the Mount of Olives and each day he taught at the temple, and the people came early in the morning to hear him.

CHAPTER 13
Wednesday & Thursday

WEDNESDAY

The Jews Plot to Kill Jesus
MT 26:1-5|MT 26:14-16|MK 14:1-2
MK 14:10-11|LK 22:1-6

When the Passover and the Feast of Unleavened Bread was only two days away, Jesus told his disciples, "The Son of Man will soon be handed over to be crucified."

The chief priests and the elders assembled in High Priest Caiaphas' palace and discussed a way to arrest Jesus and kill him. "But let's not do it during the Feast," they said, "because the people might start a riot."

Then Satan entered Judas Iscariot, one of the Twelve. Judas visited the chief priests and the temple police and asked, "What will you give me if I deliver Jesus to you?"

So they gladly gave him 30 silver coins. From then on, Judas looked for a good opportunity to betray Jesus when no crowd was present.

THURSDAY

Jesus' Disciples Prepare for the Passover
MT 26:17-20|MK 14:12-17|LK 22:7-14

On the first day of the Feast of Unleavened Bread, when the Passover lamb was normally sacrificed, Jesus told Peter and John to prepare the Passover meal.

"Where?" they asked.

"Go into the city and a man carrying a water jug will meet you. Follow him into the house he enters and tell the owner, 'The Teacher says, My appointed time is near. Where is the guest room where I can eat the Passover with my disciples?' He will take you upstairs to a large furnished room. Make preparations for us there."

The disciples went into the city and found things just as Jesus had said, and they prepared the Passover according to his instructions.

That evening Jesus arrived with the Twelve and they reclined at the table.

Jesus Washes His Disciples' Feet
JN 13:1-17

Jesus knew that the Father had put everything under his power and that the time had come for him to leave this world and return to the Father. He had loved his own, and now he showed them the full extent of his love. He got up from the meal, took off his outer clothing, and wrapped a towel around his waist. Then he poured water into a basin and began to wash his disciples' feet, drying them with the towel that was wrapped around him.

When it was Peter's turn, he said, "Lord, are you going to wash my feet?"

"You don't understand what I'm doing now, but later you will," Jesus said.

"No," said Peter, "you will never wash my feet."

"Unless I wash you, you have no part with me."

"Then, Lord, don't wash only my feet — wash my hands and my head too!"

"A person who has taken a bath only needs to wash his feet — his whole body is already clean. You are clean, but not all of you are." He said this because he knew who was going to betray him.

When he finished washing their feet, he put on his clothes and returned to the table. "Do you understand what I've done? You correctly call me Teacher and Lord. Now that I have washed your feet, follow my example and wash each other's feet. I assure you, no servant is greater than his master, nor is a messenger greater than the one who sent him. Now that you know these things, you will be blessed if you do them."

Jesus Predicts His Betrayal
MT 26:21-25|MK 14:18-21|LK 22:21-23|JN 13:18-30

Jesus then became very troubled and said, "The Scripture will soon be fulfilled: *The person who shares my bread has turned against me.* I'm not referring to all of you — I know those I've chosen. Whoever accepts anyone I send accepts me. And whoever accepts me accepts the One who sent me. I assure you, one of you here at the table is going to betray me. I'm telling you now before it happens so you will believe that I Am He."

His disciples were very sad and stared at each other, wondering who he was talking about, discussing among themselves which of them might do such a thing. Then each person asked, "Lord, it's not me is it?"

John (the disciple Jesus loved) was sitting next to Jesus. Peter motioned to him and said, "Ask him who it is."

So John leaned toward Jesus and asked, "Lord, who is it?"

"It's the person to whom I give this bread after dipping it in the dish." Then Jesus dipped the bread and gave it to Judas Iscariot, son of Simon, and said, "The Son of Man will go just as it is written about him, but woe to that person who betrays the Son of Man! It would be better for him if he had not been born."

Then Judas said, "Surely it's not me, Rabbi?"

"Yes, it is you. Go quickly and do what you've set out to do."

No one understood what was going on. Judas was in charge of the money, so some of them thought Jesus was telling him to buy what they needed for the Feast or to give something to the poor.

Satan had entered Judas as soon as he took the bread, and then Judas left room. By then it was night.

Jesus Institutes Communion
MT 26:26-29|MK 14:22-25|LK 22:15-20
JN 13:31-32|1 COR 11:25-26

Then Jesus said, "Now the Son of Man is glorified and God is glorified in him. God will glorify the Son in himself and will glorify him without delay."

While they were eating, Jesus said, "I've been looking forward to eating the Passover with you before I die; I won't eat it again until it reaches its ultimate fulfillment in God's kingdom."

He took bread, gave thanks, and broke it. Giving it to his disciples, he said, "Take and eat. This is my body given for you; do this in memory of me." After supper he took the cup of wine, gave thanks, and gave it to them. "Drink it," he said. "This establishes a new covenant and represents my blood, which is poured out for many for the forgiveness of sins. Whenever you drink this cup, do so in memory of me. I won't drink wine again until I drink it with you in my Father's kingdom. Whenever you eat this bread and drink this cup, you proclaim the Lord's death until he comes."

Jesus Predicts Peter's Denial
MT 26:31-35|MK 14:27-31|LK 22:31-34|JN 13:33-38

"I'm giving you a new command: Love each other as I have loved you. This is how everyone will know you are my disciples. I'll be with you only a little longer and I'm telling you the same thing I told the Jews: You will look for me but you can't follow me where I'm going."

"Lord, where are you going?" Peter asked.

"You can't follow me now but later you will."

"Lord, why can't I follow you now?"

"Tonight you will all desert me, for it is written: *I will strike the shepherd and the sheep of the flock will be scattered.* But after I have risen, I'll meet you in Galilee."

Peter said, "Even if everyone else deserts you, I never will."

"Simon, Simon, Satan has asked permission to sift you as wheat, but I've prayed for you, that your faith will not fail. So when you've been restored, strengthen your brothers."

"But, Lord, I'm ready to go with you to prison and to death. I'd give my life for you."

"Will you really give your life for me, Peter? I assure you that tonight, before the rooster crows twice, you will deny three times that you know me."

Peter insisted emphatically, "I'll never deny you, even if I have to die with you."

And all the other disciples said the same thing.

Jesus Comforts His Disciples
MT 26:30|MK 14:26|LK 22:35-39|JN 14:1-31

"Don't let your hearts be troubled," Jesus said. "You believe in God, believe also in me. In my Father's house are many rooms — I wouldn't tell you this if it weren't true. I'm going there to prepare a place for you, and then I'll return to bring you where I am. You know the way to where I'm going."

Thomas said, "Lord, we don't know where you're going, so how can we know the way?"

"I am the Way, the Truth, and the Life," Jesus said. "No one comes to the Father except through me. If you really know me, you know my Father also. And now not only do you know him, you have seen him."

Philip said, "Lord, show us the Father and that will be enough for us."

"Philip, I've been with you a long time. Don't you know me? Anyone who has seen me has seen the Father. So how can you ask me to show you the Father? Don't you believe I am in the Father and the Father is in me?

I'm not speaking on my own authority— it's the Father living inside me who is doing his work. Believe me when I say I am in the Father and the Father is in me, or at least believe based on the evidence of the miracles I performed. I assure you, anyone who believes in me will do the things I've been doing. And yet he will do even greater things because I'm going to the Father. And I'll do whatever you ask in my name — in this way the Son brings glory to the Father. Ask me for anything in my name and I will do it.

"If you love me, you will obey my commandments. And I'll ask the Father to give you another Comforter who will be with you forever. He is the Spirit of Truth. The world can't accept him because it can't see him and doesn't know him. But you know him because he lives with you and will be within you. I won't leave you as orphans; I will come to you. In a little while the world will no longer see me, but you will see me. Because I live, you will also live. Then you'll realize that I am in my Father, you are in me, and I am in you. Anyone who obeys my commandments demonstrates that he loves me. My Father and I will love him, and I'll reveal myself to him."

Thaddaeus asked, "Lord, why will you show yourself to us but not to the world?"

Jesus replied, "He who doesn't love me won't obey my teachings, but he who loves me will obey. My Father will love him and we'll come make our home with him. The words I speak aren't my own but are from the Father who sent me.

"I'm telling you these things while I'm still with you. But when the Father sends the Counselor — the Holy Spirit — in my name, he will teach you and remind you of everything I said. Peace I leave with you; my peace I give you. I don't give to you as the world gives.

"I told you I'm leaving, but don't be upset or afraid. I'm coming back. If you love me, you should be glad that I'm going to the Father, because the Father is greater than I. I'm telling you now before it happens, so you'll believe when it does happen. I don't have much time left to speak to you, because the ruler of this world is coming. He has no hold on me, but the world must learn that I love the Father. That's why I do exactly what he commanded me."

Then Jesus asked, "Did you lack anything when I sent you to minister without money, a backpack, or sandals?"

"No," they answered.

"But now if you have money or a backpack, take it. And if you don't have a sword, sell your coat and buy one. It is written: *He was numbered with the criminals*, and this must be fulfilled in me. Yes, what is written about me is reaching its fulfillment."

"Lord, we have two swords," the disciples said.

"That is enough," he replied. "Come, let's go."

So they sang a hymn and went out as usual to the Mount of Olives.

Jesus Is the True Vine
JN 15:1-17

As they were walking, Jesus continued, "I am the true vine and my Father is the gardener. He cuts off every branch in me that produces no fruit, but he prunes every branch that does produce, so it will be even more fruitful. You are already clean because of the things I've taught you. Remain in me and I'll remain in you. No branch can produce fruit by itself because it must remain attached to the vine. Neither can you produce fruit unless you remain in me.

"I am the vine and you are the branches. Anyone who remains in me and I in him will produce much fruit — apart from me you can do nothing. Anyone who fails to remain in me is like a branch that dries up after it has been thrown away. Such branches are gathered, thrown into the fire, and burned. If you remain in me and my words remain in you, you can ask whatever you wish and it will be given to you. It glorifies my Father when you produce much fruit, because this is how you demonstrate that you're my disciples.

"As the Father loves me, so I love you. Now remain in my love. Obey me and you will remain in my love, just as I obey my Father and remain in his love. I'm telling you this so my joy may reside in you and your joy may be complete. This is my command: Love each other as I love you. Greater love has no one than this: that he lay down his life for his friends. You are my friends if you do what I command. I no longer call you servants, because a servant doesn't know his master's business. Instead, I call you friends. I've revealed everything to you that I learned from my Father. You didn't choose me, but I chose you and appointed you to go and produce fruit that will last. Then the Father will give you whatever you ask in my name. And so I command you, love each other."

The Hatred of the World
JN 15:18-27|JN 16:1-4

"If the world hates you, remember that it hated me first. If you belonged to the world, it would love you as its own. But you don't belong to it because I called you out of it, and that's why the world hates you. Remember I told you that no servant is greater than his master. If they persecuted me, they'll persecute you also. If they obeyed my teaching, they'll obey yours also. You will be persecuted because of my name, because they don't know the One who sent me. Anyone who hates me also hates my Father. If I hadn't spoken to them and done things that no one else did, they wouldn't be guilty of sin. But now they have no excuse for their sin. Even though they saw many miracles, they hate both me and my Father. But this fulfills what is written in their Law: *They hated me for no reason.*

"I will send you the Counselor, the Spirit of Truth who goes out from the Father, and he will testify about me. You must also testify, because you've been with me from the beginning.

"I'm telling you this so you won't go astray. They will kick you out of the synagogue. In fact, a time is coming when anyone who kills you will think he's serving God. They will do these things because they don't know me and they don't know the Father. I'm telling you this so you'll remember my warnings when the time comes. I didn't tell you these things before because I was still with you."

The Holy Spirit's Role
JN 16:5-15

"But now I'm returning to him who sent me, and none of you asks where I'm going. You're sad because of what I've been saying, but I assure you that it's best for you if I go away. If I don't go, the Counselor won't come to you, but if I go I will send him to you. When he comes he will convict the world of its sin, of God's righteousness, and of the coming judgment. He will convict concerning sin because men don't believe in me; he will convict concerning God's righteousness because I'm returning to the Father and you won't see me anymore; and he will convict concerning the coming judgment because the ruler of this world has already been condemned.

"I have a lot more to say to you, but it's more than you can take right now. But when the Spirit of Truth comes, he will guide you into all truth. He won't speak on his own — he'll speak only what he hears and tell you what's yet to come. He will bring me glory by revealing to you everything he receives from me. I can say this because everything that belongs to the Father is mine."

The Disciples' Grief Will Turn to Joy
JN 16:16-33

Jesus continued, "Soon you won't see me anymore, but after a little while you'll see me again."

Some of the disciples didn't understand, so they asked each other,

"What does he mean he's going to the Father and eventually we'll see him again? What does he mean by 'a little while'?"

Jesus knew they wanted to question him, so he said, "Are you wondering what I meant? I assure you, the world will rejoice while you weep and mourn. You will grieve but your grief will turn to joy. A woman experiences pain when she gives birth, but because of her joy, she forgets the pain when her baby arrives. In the same way, this is your time of grief, but I will see you again and you will rejoice, and no one will take away your joy. Then you won't need to ask me for anything because, I assure you, my Father will give you whatever you ask in my name. You haven't yet asked for anything in my name, but ask and you will receive and your joy will be complete.

"I've been speaking figuratively, but soon I will speak plainly about my Father. At that time you will ask in my name. It won't be necessary for me to ask the Father on your behalf, because the Father himself loves you since you love me and believe I came from God. I came from the Father and entered the world, and now I'm leaving the world and returning to the Father."

Jesus' disciples said, "Now you're speaking clearly and not figuratively. Clearly you know everything and you don't need anyone to question you. This is why we believe that you came from God."

"Finally, you believe!" Jesus replied. "But a time is coming, in fact has now come, when each of you will be scattered to his own home. You'll leave me all alone, but I'm not alone, because my Father is with me.

"I told you these things so that in me you will have peace. In this world you will have trouble. But be encouraged! I have overcome the world."

Jesus Prays for Himself
JN 17:1-5

Then Jesus looked toward heaven and prayed, "Father, the time has now come. Glorify your Son so your Son may glorify you. You gave him authority over all people so that he might give eternal life to those you gave to him. Now this is eternal life: that they know you — the only true God — and Jesus Christ, whom you sent. I brought you glory on earth by completing the work you gave me to do. Now Father, glorify me in your presence with the glory I shared with you before the world began."

Jesus Prays for His Disciples
JN 17:6-19

"Father, I revealed you to those you took out of the world. They were yours but you gave them to me, and they obeyed you. Now they know that everything I have comes from you. I gave them the words you gave me, and they accepted them. They truly understand that I came from you and believe that you sent me. I'm not praying for the world, but I pray for those you gave me because they are yours. All I have is yours and all you have is mine. I have been glorified in them. I won't be in the world much longer because I'm returning to you, but they're still in the world. Holy Father, protect them by the power of your name — the name you gave me — so they may be one as we are one. While I was with them, I protected them and kept them safe by the name you gave me. None of them is lost except the one destined for destruction, in fulfillment of Scripture.

"I'm coming to you now, but I'm saying these things while I'm still here so that my disciples may have the full measure of my joy within them. I gave them your word, and the world hates them because they are not of the world any more than I am of the world. I'm not praying that you take them out of the world but that you protect them from the evil one. Sanctify them by your word, which is truth. Just as you sent me into the world, I sent them into the world. I sanctify myself for them so they too may be truly sanctified."

Jesus Prays for All Believers
JN 17:20-26

"I'm not praying just for my disciples; I pray also for those who will believe in me through their message, so that all of them may be one, Father, just as you are in me and I am in you. May they also be in us so the world will believe you sent me. I gave them the glory you gave to me so they will be one as we are one: I in them and you in me. May they be completely one so the world will know that you sent me and that you love them even as you love me.

"Father, I want those you gave me to be with me where I am so they can see my glory, which you gave me, because you loved me before the creation of the world. Righteous Father, even though the world doesn't know you, I know you, and these believers know that you sent me. I made you known to them and will continue to make you known so that the love you have for me will be in them and I myself will be in them."

Jesus Prays on the Mount of Olives
MT 26:36-46|MK 14:32-42|LK 22:40-46|JN 18:1

When Jesus finished praying, he and his disciples crossed the Kidron Valley. On the other side they went into an olive grove, which was in a garden called Gethsemane.

Then Jesus said, "Pray that you won't fall into temptation."

Then he withdrew about a stone's throw beyond them, taking Peter, James, and John with him.

Deeply distressed and troubled, Jesus said to them, "My heart is breaking with grief, to the point that I can hardly bear it. Stay here and keep watch with me."

He went a little farther, fell with his face to the ground, and prayed, "Abba, Father, everything is possible for you. Take this cup from me if you are willing, yet not my will but yours be done."

When he returned, he found the disciples asleep. They were very tired and exhausted from sorrow.

"Couldn't you keep watch with me for one hour?" he asked Peter. "Watch and pray so you won't fall into temptation. The spirit is willing, but the body is weak."

He left them again and prayed, "My Father, if it's not possible for this cup to be taken away unless I drink it, may your will be done."

He returned again and found the disciples sleeping, and they didn't know what to say.

Jesus went and prayed the same prayer a third time. In his anguish he prayed more intensely, his sweat falling to the ground like drops of blood. Then an angel appeared and strengthened him.

When Jesus returned he asked the disciples, "Are you still sleeping? Let's go. It's time! My betrayer is coming to turn the Son of Man over into the hands of sinners."

Judas Betrays Jesus With a Kiss
MT 26:47-50a|MK 14:43-45|LK 22:47-48|JN 18:2-9

Now Judas knew the garden's location because Jesus often met there with his disciples. He arrived while Jesus was still speaking, guiding a detachment of soldiers and officials who were armed with swords and clubs and carrying torches and lanterns. The chief priests, the teachers of the law, the Pharisees, and the elders had sent them.

Judas had told the men, "The one I kiss is the man; arrest him and lead him away under guard." So Judas approached Jesus and said, "Greetings, Rabbi!" And then he kissed him.

"Friend, do what you came for," Jesus said. "Are you betraying the Son of Man with a kiss?"

Jesus knew everything that was going to happen to him, so he stepped forward and asked them, "Who are you looking for?"

"Jesus of Nazareth," they replied.

"I Am He."

And they drew back and fell to the ground. Judas, the betrayer, was standing there with them.

"Who is it you want?" Jesus asked again.

"Jesus of Nazareth."

"I told you that I Am He. Since you want me, let these men go."

This happened so his words would be fulfilled: "I haven't lost any of those you gave me."

Peter Cuts Off Malchus' Ear
MT 26:50b-54|MK 14:46a|MK 14:47
LK 22:49-51|JN 18:10-11

Then the men stepped forward and grabbed Jesus.

One of the disciples asked, "Lord, should we use our swords?" Then Peter drew his sword and cut off the right ear of the high priest's servant, Malchus.

"Enough!" Jesus commanded Peter. "Put your sword away, for all who draw the sword will die by the sword. Don't you know I can call on my Father and he'll immediately send more than 12 legions of angels? But if I don't drink the cup the Father has given me, how would the Scriptures be fulfilled that say it must happen this way?"

So Jesus touched Malchus' ear and healed him.

Jesus Is Arrested
MT 26:55-56|MK 14:46b|MK 14:48-52
LK 22:52-53|JN 18:12

Jesus said to those who were with Judas, "Did you come with swords and clubs to capture me as if I'm leading a rebellion? I taught in the temple courts every day and you didn't touch me, but this is your hour — when darkness reigns. All of this is happening to fulfill the writings of the prophets."

Then the soldiers and the Jewish officials arrested Jesus and tied him up, and all the disciples ran away and deserted him. A young man wearing only a linen garment was also following Jesus. The men grabbed him but he ran away naked, leaving his garment behind.

Annas Questions Jesus
MT 26:58a|MK 14:54a|LK 22:54
JN 18:13-16|JN 18:19-23

The soldiers took Jesus to Annas, who was the father-in-law of Caiaphas, who was high priest that year. Caiaphas is the one who had advised the Jews it would be beneficial if one man died for the people.

Now Peter and John followed Jesus at a distance. The high priest knew John and allowed him to go with Jesus into the high priest's courtyard, but

Peter waited outside. Then John came back, spoke to the girl on duty, and brought Peter in.

Meanwhile, Annas questioned Jesus about his disciples and his teachings.

"I spoke openly to the world," Jesus replied. "I always taught in the synagogues or at the temple, where all the Jews meet. I didn't say anything secretly. Why question me? Ask those who heard me — surely they know what I said."

One of the officials hit Jesus in the face. "Is this how you speak to the high priest?"

"If I said something wrong, tell me what it was. But if I spoke the truth, why did you hit me?"

Peter Denies Jesus
MT 26:58b|MT 26:69-75|MK 14:54b|MK 14:66-72
LK 22:55-62|JN 18:17-18|JN 18:25-27

It was cold, so the servants and officials started a fire in the middle of the courtyard and sat down. And Peter sat with them.

The First Denial

One of the high priest's servant girls saw Peter sitting in the firelight. She looked at him closely and said, "You were also with that Nazarene, Jesus. Aren't you one of his disciples?"

"I don't know what you're talking about," Peter said.

The Second Denial

Then he went out into the entryway. The servant girl saw him again and said to those standing around, "He's one of them."

Peter denied it with an oath: "I don't know the man!"

The Third Denial

About an hour later, one of the high priest's servants saw Peter. "Didn't I see you with Jesus in the olive grove?" the servant asked. He was a relative of Malchus, whose ear Peter had cut off.

Peter denied it again, but the people standing there said, "Your Galilean accent gives you away — you must be one of his disciples!"

And Peter began to call down curses on himself, and he swore, "Listen, I don't know this man you're talking about!"

And the rooster crowed just as he was speaking.

Then Jesus turned around and looked straight at Peter. And Peter remembered that Jesus had said, "Before the rooster crows today, you will deny me three times," and he went outside and wept inconsolably.

CHAPTER 14
Friday & Saturday

FRIDAY

Jesus Stands Trial Before the Sanhedrin
MT 26:57|MT 26:59-68|MK 14:53
MK 14:55-65|LK 22:63-71|JN 18:24

In the morning Annas sent Jesus, still tied up, to Caiaphas the high priest. Members of the Sanhedrin — which consisted of the chief priests, elders, and teachers of the law — had gathered there. They were looking for evidence against Jesus so they could sentence him to death, but they didn't find any.

Some people stated, "We heard him say, 'I'll destroy this man-made temple and in three days build another, not made by man.'"

Others testified falsely against him, but their statements didn't agree.

Then Caiaphas stood up and asked Jesus, "Aren't you going to respond? What do you have to say about the testimony of these men?"

But Jesus didn't answer.

"Are you the Christ, the Son of the Blessed One?"

Jesus replied, "If I tell you, you won't believe me. And if I ask you a question, you won't answer."

Caiaphas said, "You are under oath! I command you to answer in the name of the living God! Are you the Christ? Are you the Son of God?"

"Yes, it's just as you say. And in the future you will see the Son of Man sitting at the right hand of the Mighty One, coming on the clouds of heaven."

Then Caiaphas tore his clothes. "We don't we need any more witnesses," he told the Jewish leaders. "You heard the blasphemy from his own lips, so what do you think?"

"He should be put to death," they said.

Then the men guarding Jesus mocked him. They blindfolded him, spit in his face, and punched him. Others slapped him and said, "Prophesy, Christ — who hit you?" And they also said many other insulting things.

Judas was sorry when he saw that Jesus had been condemned, so he took the 30 silver coins back to the chief priests and the elders in the temple. "I've sinned," he said. "I betrayed innocent blood."

"What does that have to do with us?" they replied. "That's your problem."

Then Judas threw the money on the floor and went and hanged himself.

The chief priests said, "This is blood money; therefore it's against the law to put it into the treasury."

So they decided to use money, the reward Judas had received for his wickedness, to buy the potter's field as a burial place for foreigners. Judas had fallen there on his head — his body burst open and his intestines spilled out. When the people in Jerusalem heard about it, they called the field *Akeldama,* which means *field of blood* in their language. So Jeremiah's prophecy was fulfilled: *They took the 30 silver coins — the price set on him by the people of Israel — and used them to buy the potter's field, as the Lord commanded me.*

Then the Jewish leaders tied Jesus up and took him to the Roman governor's palace, where they delivered him to Pilate. The Jews wanted to be able to eat the Passover meal, so they stayed outside the palace to avoid ceremonial uncleanness. It was still early in the morning as Jesus stood before the governor.

Pilate came out and asked, "What charges are you bringing against this man?"

"We wouldn't have brought him to you if he weren't a criminal," they replied. "He's been disrupting our nation. He's against paying taxes to Caesar and claims to be Christ, a king!"

"Judge him by your own law then."

"We don't have the right to execute anyone," the Jews objected.

This fulfilled Jesus' prophecy about how he would die.

Pilate took Jesus inside the palace and asked, "Are you the king of the Jews?"

"Are you asking this on your own or did you hear it from others?"

"I'm not a Jew, am I?" Pilate asked. "Your own people and chief priests brought you to me. What have you done?"

"My kingdom is not of this world. If it were, my servants would have fought to prevent me from being arrested. My kingdom is from another place."

"So you are a king then!" Pilate said.

"You're correct that I am a king. The reason I was born and the reason I came into the world is to testify to the truth. Everyone who loves the truth listens to me."

"What is truth?" Pilate asked.

Then they went back outside. Pilate told the Jews, "I don't believe he's done anything wrong."

So the chief priests and the elders began to accuse Jesus again.

"Don't you hear all their accusations?" Pilate asked Jesus. "Aren't you going to say anything?"

But Jesus didn't respond to a single charge, and Pilate was amazed.

"He stirs up everyone with his teaching, from Galilee to Judea," the Jews continued, "and now he has come all the way here!"

Pilate Sends Jesus to Herod
LK 23:6-12

When Pilate found out Jesus was a Galilean, he realized that Jesus was under Herod's jurisdiction. Since Herod was in Jerusalem, Pilate sent Jesus to him.

Herod was very happy to see Jesus because he had wanted to meet him for a long time. He had heard a lot about him and hoped he would perform a miracle. Herod asked many questions, but Jesus didn't respond. And the chief priests and the teachers of the law passionately accused him. Herod and his soldiers teased and insulted him, and then they dressed him in an elegant robe and sent him back to Pilate. Herod and Pilate had previously been enemies, but that day they became friends.

Pilate Tries to Release Jesus
MT 27:15-23|MT 27:27-30|MK 15:6-14|MK 15:16-19
LK 23:13-22|JN 18:39-40|JN 19:1-15

While Pilate was sitting on the judge's seat, his wife sent him a message: "Don't have anything to do with that innocent man; I've suffered terribly today because of a dream I had about him."

Then Pilate gathered the chief priests, the leaders, and the people and said, "You accused Jesus of starting a rebellion, but I examined him in your presence and find no crime for which to charge him. Herod didn't find anything either and sent him back. Obviously he has done nothing to deserve the death penalty."

Pilate knew they had brought Jesus to him because they were jealous, so he said, "It's your custom to choose a prisoner to release at the Passover. Should I release Barabbas or Jesus, who is called Christ — the King of the Jews?"

Barabbas was an infamous criminal who was in prison with those who had committed murder during the rebellion.

The chief priests and the elders had persuaded the people to have Jesus executed. So the crowd shouted, "Don't release Jesus! Take him away and release Barabbas!"

"Then what should I do with Jesus?" Pilate asked.

"Crucify him!"

Pilate wanted to release Jesus, so he appealed to them again. But they kept shouting, "Crucify him! Crucify him!"

"Why?" Pilate asked. "What has he done wrong? I find no grounds for the death penalty. I'll have him whipped and then release him."

Pilate gave the order and his soldiers took Jesus into the palace (also known as the Praetorium) and called the whole company of soldiers together. They stripped him and dressed him in a purple robe, and then they put a reed in his right hand as a staff. They made a crown of thorns and put it on Jesus' head. "Hail, king of the Jews," they taunted repeatedly. They spit on him, slapped him, and kept hitting him on the head with the reed. Then they fell on their knees and pretended to worship him.

Pilate brought Jesus out wearing the crown of thorns and the purple robe and said, "Look, here is the man! I'm bringing him out to show you that I find him guilty of no crime."

The chief priests and temple officials shouted, "Crucify! Crucify!"

"You crucify him then. I find him guilty of no crime."

"According to our law he must die, because he claimed to be the Son of God."

That made Pilate even more afraid. He took Jesus back inside the palace and asked, "Where do you come from?"

Jesus didn't respond.

"Are you refusing to speak to me?" Pilate asked. "Don't you know I have the power to free you or to crucify you?"

"You would have no power over me if it hadn't been given to you from above. Therefore those who delivered me to you are guilty of a greater sin."

Pilate continued trying to release Jesus, but the Jews shouted, "You'll be an enemy of Caesar if you let him go. Anyone who claims to be a king opposes Caesar."

It was now almost 6am on the day of preparation for the Passover. Pilate brought Jesus out and sat on the judge's seat, also known as the Stone Pavement (*Gabbatha* in Hebrew). "Here is your king," he said.

"Take him away! Take him away! Crucify him!" they shouted.

"Should I crucify your king?"

"We have no king but Caesar," the chief priests said.

Pilate Sentences Jesus to Death
MT 27:24-26|MK 15:15|LK 23:23-25|JN 19:16a

When Pilate realized he wasn't getting anywhere and that a riot was starting, he washed his hands in front of the crowd. "I'm innocent of this man's blood," he said. "It's your responsibility!"

The people answered, "Let his blood be on us and on our children!"

So Pilate satisfied the crowd and released Barabbas, who had been put in prison for rebellion and murder, but he had Jesus whipped and handed him over to be crucified.

Simon of Cyrene Carries Jesus' Cross
MT 27:31-32|MK 15:20-21|LK 23:26|JN 19:16b-17a

The soldiers ridiculed Jesus, stripped the purple robe off him, and dressed him in his own clothes. Then they led him away to crucify him, making him carry his own cross.

A Cyrenian named Simon, the father of Alexander and Rufus, passed by on his way in from the country. The soldiers grabbed Simon, laid the cross on him, and forced him to carry it behind Jesus.

Women Mourn for Jesus
LK 23:27-31

A crowd followed, including women who were mourning and crying. Jesus turned and said, "Daughters of Jerusalem, don't cry for me; cry for yourselves and for your children. The time is coming when you'll say, 'Blessed are childless women — the wombs that never bore and breasts that never nursed!' Then everyone will plead with the mountains, 'Fall on us!' and with the hills, 'Cover us!' For if men do these things when the tree is green, what will happen when it is dry?"

Jesus Is Crucified
MT 27:33-34|MT 27:38|MK 15:22-23|MK 15:25
MK 15:27-28|LK 23:32-34a|JN 19:17b-18

Two criminals were also led out with Jesus to be crucified. They arrived at *Golgotha,* a Hebrew name meaning *skull place.*

The soldiers gave Jesus wine mixed with myrrh, but when he tasted it he refused to drink it.

It was about 9am when they crucified Jesus, with one criminal on his right and the other on his left. This fulfilled the Scripture, *He was counted among the criminals.*

Then Jesus said, "Father, forgive them; they don't know what they're doing."

The Soldiers Cast Lots for Jesus' Clothing
MT 27:35-36|MK 15:24|LK 23:34b|JN 19:23-24

The soldiers divided Jesus' clothing into four parts, one for each of them. But the undergarment was seamless, woven in one piece from top to bottom. "Don't tear it," they said. "Let's cast lots to determine who will receive it." So the Scripture was fulfilled: *They divided my garments among themselves and cast lots for my clothing.*

Afterward the soldiers sat down and guarded Jesus.

Pilate Hangs a Sign on Jesus' Cross
MT 27:37|MK 15:26|LK 23:38|JN 19:19-22

Pilate hung a sign on the cross above Jesus' head identifying the charge against him: *This is Jesus the Nazarene, the king of the Jews.* It was written in Aramaic, Latin, and Greek and many people saw it because Jesus was crucified near the city.

But the chief priests protested and said to Pilate, "Don't write that he *is* the king of the Jews but that he *claimed* to be king of the Jews."

Pilate answered, "What I have written, I have written."

The Crowd Insults Jesus
MT 27:39-43|MK 15:29-32a|LK 23:35

People passing by shook their heads and shouted at Jesus, "Since you said you'd destroy the temple and rebuild it in three days, save yourself! Come down from the cross if you're the Son of God!"

The chief priests and the teachers of the law said to each other, "He saved others but he can't save himself! Let's see him come down from the cross if he's God's Messiah, the king of Israel. Then we'll believe in him. He trusts in God so let God rescue him now, if he wants him. After all, he claimed to be the Son of God."

Jesus Saves the Repentant Criminal
MT 27:44|MK 15:32b|LK 23:39-43

One of the criminals who had also been crucified said to Jesus, "Aren't you the Messiah? Save yourself and us!"

But the other criminal said, "You're under the same sentence — don't you fear God? We're getting what we deserve for our actions, but this man has done nothing wrong." Then he said to Jesus, "Remember me when you come into your kingdom."

"I assure you, today you will be with me in paradise," Jesus said.

Jesus Entrusts His Mother to John
JN 19:25a|JN 19:26-27

Jesus' mother and John (the disciple Jesus loved) were standing near the cross. And Jesus said to his mother, "Dear woman, that is your son." To John he said, "That is your mother."

And from then on she lived with John in his home.

Jesus Gives Up His Spirit
MT 27:45-50|MK 15:33-37|LK 23:36-37
LK 23:44-45a|LK 23:46|JN 19:28-30

From noon until 3pm, the sun stopped shining and darkness covered the entire land. At 3pm Jesus shouted, *"Eloi, Eloi, lama sabachthani?"* — which means, *My God, my God, why have you forsaken me?*

Some people standing there said, "Listen, he's calling for Elijah."

Jesus knew that everything had been completed. In fulfillment of Scripture he said, "I'm thirsty."

Someone ran to get a sponge, and the soldiers soaked it in a jar of sour wine, put it on a stalk of hyssop, and lifted it to Jesus' lips.

"Save yourself if you're the king of the Jews," they said.

Others said, "Now leave him alone. Let's see if Elijah comes to save him."

After drinking the wine, Jesus shouted, "It is finished! Father, into your hands I commit my spirit."

Then he hung his head and gave up his spirit.

Supernatural Events Occur After Jesus' Death
MT 27:51-54|MK 15:38-39|LK 23:45b|LK 23:47

Immediately, the curtain of the temple split in two from top to bottom. An earthquake broke the rocks apart and tombs opened up and the saints who had died were raised — they appeared to many people in Jerusalem after Jesus' resurrection.

When the centurion and the others who were guarding Jesus saw the earthquake, how Jesus died, and everything else that had happened, they were terrified.

The centurion glorified God and said, "He was a righteous man. He really was the Son of God!"

Jesus' Friends and Family Mourn
MT 27:55-56|MK 15:40-41|LK 23:48-49|JN 19:25b

The people who had witnessed Jesus' death beat their chests in deep sorrow and regret, and then they left, but those who knew him well stood watching at a distance. Among them were:

* **Mary Magdalene**
* **Mary**, the wife of Clopas and mother of Joseph and James the younger
* **Salome**, the wife of Zebedee and mother of James and John. She was also Jesus' aunt — his mother's sister.

They had followed Jesus from Galilee to tend to his needs. Many other women were present who had traveled with Jesus to Jerusalem.

Jesus' Side Is Pierced
JN 19:31-37

It was Preparation Day (the day before the Sabbath). The Jews didn't want the bodies left on the crosses, because the next day was a special Sabbath. So the soldiers got permission from Pilate to have the men's legs broken and the bodies taken down. The soldiers broke the legs of both the men who had been crucified with Jesus, but they didn't break Jesus' legs because he was already dead. Instead, a soldier pierced his side with a spear and blood and water flowed out. So the Scripture was fulfilled: *Not one of his bones will be broken* and *They will look upon the one they pierced*.

The disciple John witnessed this, so he knows that it's true. He testifies so that you also may believe.

Joseph of Arimathea and Nicodemus Claim Jesus' Body
MT 27:57-61|MK 15:42-47|LK 23:50-56|JN 19:38-42

There was a rich man named Joseph who was from Arimathea in Judea. Although he was a prominent member of the Sanhedrin, he was a righteous man and hadn't agreed with their actions. He was looking forward to the kingdom of God but followed Jesus' secretly because he was afraid of the Jews.

That evening he boldly asked Pilate if he could remove Jesus' body. Pilate was surprised that Jesus was already dead, so he sent the centurion to confirm it. Then he allowed Joseph to take the body.

Nicodemus, who had visited Jesus at night, assisted Joseph. He brought a 75-pound mixture of myrrh and aloes, and Joseph bought a clean cloth made of fine linen. They wrapped Jesus' body with the fragrant spices in strips of linen, in accordance with Jewish burial customs.

Joseph had carved himself a new tomb out of a rock and it was in a garden near the crucifixion site. No one had ever been buried in it. Since it was preparation day and the Sabbath was about to begin, and because the tomb was nearby, they buried Jesus there. Then they rolled a large stone in front of the tomb's entrance, and they left.

Mary Magdalene, Mary the wife of Clopas, and the other women from Galilee sat across from the tomb and watched as Jesus was buried. Afterward they went home and prepared spices and perfumes. Then they rested on the Sabbath in obedience to the commandment.

SATURDAY

Soldiers Guard the Tomb
MT 27:62-66

The next day was the Sabbath, and the chief priests and the Pharisees visited Pilate.

"Sir," they said, "while that deceiver was alive, he said he would rise again in three days. So order the tomb to be made secure until the third day. Otherwise his disciples might steal the body and tell people he has risen from the dead. That would be a worst deception than the first one!"

"Take some guards and make the tomb as secure as you can," Pilate said.

So they put a seal on the stone and posted soldiers as guards.

PART VI

JESUS' RESURRECTION AND ASCENSION

CHAPTER 15
Resurrection Sunday

The Women Visit Jesus' Tomb
MT 28:1-8|MK 16:1-8|LK 24:1-8|LK 24:10|JN 20:1

When the Sabbath was over, just before dawn on Sunday, there was a violent earthquake. An angel of the Lord came down from heaven, rolled the stone away from the tomb, and sat on it. His appearance was like lightning and his clothes were white as snow. The guards trembled with fear and became as still as dead men.

Mary Magdalene, Mary the wife of Clopas, Salome, Joanna, and the other women took the spices they had prepared and started for the tomb to anoint Jesus' body. It was still dark and they asked each other, "Who will roll the stone away from the tomb entrance?" But when they arrived, the large stone had already been rolled away.

They entered the tomb, but Jesus' body wasn't there! While they were wondering what had happened, two angels wearing clothes as bright as lightning suddenly appeared. One stood beside them and the other sat on the right side of the tomb in a long, white robe. The women were amazed and terrified, and they bowed down before the angels.

One of the angels said, "Don't be afraid; you're looking for Jesus the Nazarene, who was crucified. But why are you looking for the living among the dead? He's not here — he has risen just as he said. Look at the place where he lay. Remember in Galilee he told you, 'The Son of Man must be delivered into the hands of sinful men, be crucified, and rise on the third day.'"

Then the women remembered what Jesus had said.

"Go quickly and tell his disciples, and Peter, that he has risen from the dead and will meet you in Galilee. You will see him there, just as he said."

So the women quickly ran out of the tomb trembling, afraid but also overwhelmed with joy and amazement. They said nothing to anyone as they ran to share the news with Jesus' disciples.

The Guards Report the Empty Tomb
MT 28:11-15

While the women were on their way, some of the guards went into the city and told the chief priests everything that had happened. The chief priests met with the elders and devised a plan. They paid the soldiers generously and told them to say that Jesus' disciples had stolen the body during the night while they were asleep. "If the governor hears about this, we'll handle him and keep you out of trouble," they promised.

So the soldiers took the money and did as they were instructed. And their story has been spread among the Jews to this day.

Peter and John Race to the Tomb
MK 16:10|LK 24:9|LK 24:11-12|JN 20:2-9

While the 11 disciples and other followers were mourning and weeping, the women arrived and Mary Magdalene said, "They've taken the Lord from the tomb and we don't know where they put him!"

The disciples didn't believe the women because what they said sounded like nonsense. But Peter and John (the disciple Jesus loved) ran to the tomb. John outran Peter and arrived first. He looked in and saw the strips of linen lying there, but he didn't go in. Then Peter arrived and went inside the tomb. He saw the strips of linen and the burial cloth that had been wrapped around Jesus' head. The cloth was not with the linen but was folded up by itself. When Peter saw this, he was amazed. Then John entered the tomb. He saw the burial clothing and believed. But they still didn't understand from Scripture that Jesus had to rise from the dead.

Jesus Appears to Mary Magdalene and Other Women
MT 28:9-10|MK 16:9|MK 16:11|JN 20:10-18

The disciples left, but Mary and the other women stayed behind. As Mary stood outside the tomb crying, she saw two angels dressed in white. They were sitting where Jesus' body had been, one at the head and the other at the foot.

"Why are you crying?" they asked.

"Because they took my Lord away and I don't know where they put him."

Then she turned around and saw Jesus standing there, but she didn't recognize him.

"Woman, why are you crying?" he asked. "Who are you looking for?"

Mary thought he was the gardener so she said, "Sir, if you took Jesus body, tell me where he is and I'll come get him."

"Mary," Jesus said.

She said in Aramaic, *"Rabboni!"* (This means Teacher.)

"Greetings," Jesus said to Mary and the other women.

Then they grabbed his feet and worshiped him.

"Don't hold on to me, because I haven't yet ascended to the Father. Now go tell my brothers, my disciples, that I'm returning to my Father and your Father, to my God and your God, but I will meet them in Galilee."

So Mary Magdalene went and told the disciples, "I've seen the Lord!" She told them everything he had said to her, but they didn't believe that Jesus was alive and that she had seen him.

Jesus Appears to Two Disciples on the Road to Emmaus
MK 16:12-13|LK 24:13-35

That same day Cleopas and another of Jesus' followers traveled to Emmaus, a village about seven miles from Jerusalem. As they discussed everything that had happened, Jesus joined them and walked with them, but they were prevented from recognizing him.

"What are you discussing?" Jesus asked.

They stopped walking, looking discouraged. Cleopas asked, "Are you the only visitor in Jerusalem who doesn't know about the things that have happened?"

"What things?"

"Jesus of Nazareth was a prophet, confirmed by God and considered by all the people to be a powerful preacher and miracle worker. Our chief priests and leaders delivered him to be sentenced to death, and they crucified him, but we hoped he'd be the one to redeem Israel. Not only that, but this is the third day since everything has happened. Some women from our group went to the tomb early this morning but didn't find Jesus' body. They amazed us, saying they had seen angels who told them he was alive! Some of the disciples went to the tomb and found it just as the women had said — they didn't see Jesus either."

Jesus replied, "How unwise you are, and how slow you are to believe everything the prophets said! Didn't the Christ have to suffer and enter into his glory?" Then Jesus began with Moses and the Prophets and explained what the Scriptures said about himself.

As they approached Emmaus, Jesus gave the impression that he would continue to travel. But the disciples begged him, "Stay with us. The day is fading; it's almost evening."

So Jesus stayed with them. At the table he gave thanks, broke the bread, and gave it to them. Then their eyes were opened and they recognized him. Afterward he disappeared right before their eyes.

"Weren't our hearts burning within us while he talked with us on the road and explained the Scriptures?" they said.

They returned to Jerusalem immediately, where the disciples and the others told them, "It's all true! The Lord has risen and he appeared to Peter."

Then the two disciples told what had happened as they traveled to Emmaus, and how they had recognized Jesus when he broke bread.

Jesus Appears to His Apostles
MK 16:14|LK 24:36-43|JN 20:19-23

The disciples gathered that Sunday evening, and they locked the doors because they were afraid of the Jews.

Jesus appeared while they were at the table and said, "Peace be with you!"

The disciples were surprised and frightened because they thought he was a ghost.

Jesus admonished them for their lack of faith and their stubborn refusal to believe those who had seen him after he had risen. "Why are you anxious and why do you have doubts?" he asked. "Look at my hands and feet. It's really me! Touch me and see — a ghost doesn't have flesh and bones like I do."

When he showed them his hands and feet, they were so happy and amazed that they still couldn't believe it.

Then Jesus asked, "Do you have anything to eat?"

They gave him a piece of broiled fish, and he ate it before their eyes.

"Peace be with you!" Jesus said again. "I'm sending you just as the Father sent me." Then he breathed on them and said, "Receive the Holy Spirit. If you forgive anyone's sins, they are forgiven; if you don't forgive them, they are not forgiven."

CHAPTER 16
Jesus' Farewell to His Disciples

Jesus Appears to Thomas
JN 20:24-29

Thomas wasn't present when Jesus appeared, so the other disciples told him, "We saw the Lord!"

But Thomas said, "I won't believe unless I touch his side and feel the nail scars in his hands."

Eight days later, the disciples were together again, and this time Thomas was with them. Even though the doors were locked, Jesus appeared and said, "Peace be with you!" Then he said to Thomas, "Look at my hands. Feel the nail scars and touch my side. Stop doubting and believe."

"My Lord and my God!" Thomas said.

"You believe because you can see me — blessed are those who haven't seen me, yet they believe."

The Great Catch of Fish on the Sea of Galilee
JN 21:1-14

Some time later in Galilee, Peter, Thomas, Nathanael, James, John, and two other disciples were together.

"I'm going fishing," Peter said.

"We'll go with you."

So they went out on the boat that night on the Sea of Galilee, but they didn't catch anything. Early in the morning Jesus appeared on the shore, but the disciples didn't recognize him.

"Friends, do you have any fish?" Jesus asked.

"No," they answered.

"Cast the net on the right side of the boat and you'll find some."

When they did, they were unable to haul in the net because it held so many fish.

"It's the Lord!" John (the disciple Jesus loved) told Peter.

Peter picked up the outer garment he had taken off and wrapped it around himself. Then he jumped into the sea. The other disciples followed in the boat, towing the net full of fish. They were only about 100 yards from the shore and when they arrived, they saw that Jesus had some bread and a fire of burning coals with fish cooking on it.

"Bring some of the fish you caught," Jesus said.

So Peter got back in the boat and dragged the net to the shore. It was filled with 153 large fish, but the net wasn't torn.

"Come have breakfast," Jesus said. Then he gave them some bread and fish.

None of the disciples dared to ask, "Who are you?" They knew it was the Lord. This was the third time Jesus had appeared to his disciples after he had risen from the dead.

Jesus Restores Peter
JN 21:15-23

When they finished eating, Jesus said, "Simon, son of John, do you love me more than these?"

"Yes, Lord," Peter said, "you know I love you."

"Then feed my lambs."

Jesus asked again, "Simon, son of John, do you love me?"

"Yes, Lord, you know I love you."

"Take care of my sheep."

Jesus asked yet again, "Simon, son of John, do you love me?"

Peter was hurt because Jesus asked him the same question three times. "Lord, you know everything — you know I love you."

"Then feed my sheep. When you were young, you dressed yourself and went wherever you wanted to go. But I assure you that when you grow old, you'll stretch out your hands and someone else will dress you and take you where you don't want to go." Jesus said this to indicate the kind of death by which Peter would glorify God. Then he said, "Follow me!"

Now John was following them. He's the same disciple who had leaned against Jesus at the Passover meal and asked which of them would betray him.

Peter turned and saw John and asked, "Lord, what about him?"

"If I want him to remain alive until I return, what does that have to do with you?" Jesus replied. "You must follow me."

So a rumor spread among the disciples that John wouldn't die, but that's not what Jesus had said.

Later the 11 disciples, along with 500 others, traveled to the mountain in Galilee where Jesus had told them to go. Some people worshiped Jesus when they saw him, but others hesitated.

Jesus approached them and said, "All authority in heaven and on earth has been given to me. Go and make disciples of all nations. Baptize them in the name of the Father and of the Son and of the Holy Spirit, and teach them to obey everything I commanded you. Whoever believes and is baptized will be saved, but whoever doesn't believe will be condemned. These are the signs that will accompany those who believe: They will drive out demons in my name; they will speak in new languages; they will pick up snakes; they will touch the sick and heal them, and if they drink deadly poison, it won't hurt them."

Then Jesus led the disciples to the Mount of Olives, near Bethany, and he opened their minds so they could understand the Scriptures. "Remember I told you that everything written about me in the Law of Moses, the Prophets, and the Psalms must be fulfilled: The Christ will suffer and rise from the dead on the third day, and repentance and forgiveness of sins will be preached in his name to all nations, beginning in Jerusalem. You are witnesses of these things. I'm going to send you what my Father promised. John baptized with water, but in a few days you will be baptized with the Holy Spirit. Stay in Jerusalem until you've been clothed with power from on high."

"Lord," they asked, "are you going to restore the kingdom to Israel at that time?"

"It's not for you to know the times or dates the Father has set by his own authority. But you will receive power when the Holy Spirit comes upon you, and you will be my witnesses in Jerusalem, Judea, Samaria, and to the ends of the earth. And remember I am with you always, until the very end of the age."

Then Jesus lifted his hands. As he blessed them, he was taken up before their eyes, and a cloud concealed him and carried him away into heaven.

As the disciples stood gazing into the sky, two angels dressed in white suddenly appeared. "Men of Galilee," they said, "why are you standing there looking up into heaven? This same Jesus, who has been taken from you into heaven, will come back just as you saw him go."

The disciples worshiped Jesus and were filled with joy. They traveled a Sabbath's day journey to Jerusalem, where they praised God continually at the temple.

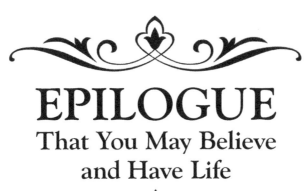

EPILOGUE
That You May Believe and Have Life

MK 16:9a|MK 16:19b-20|JN 20:30-31
JN 21:24-25|1 COR 15:5-7|ACTS 1:3

When Jesus rose early on Sunday morning, he appeared to Mary Magdalene and several other women. He then appeared to Peter and later to all the apostles. Afterward he appeared to more than 500 of the brothers at the same time; some of them have passed away, but most are still living. Later he appeared to his brother, James.

Jesus appeared to his disciples over a period of 40 days, providing abundant evidence that he was alive and teaching them about the kingdom of God. Then he was taken up into heaven, where he sat at the right hand of God. His disciples preached everywhere, and the Lord worked with them and confirmed his word by the signs that accompanied it.

John the disciple testifies to these things and wrote them down. We know that his testimony is true. Jesus performed many other miracles in the presence of his disciples that aren't recorded in this book. If all of them were written down, the whole world wouldn't have room for the books that would be written. But these things are written so that you may believe that Jesus is the Christ, the Son of God, and that by believing you may have life in his name.

About C. Austin Tucker

C. Austin Tucker is a writer, editor, and teacher with a passion for God and his Word. She has been a Bible teacher for more than 15 years and is the founder of Route 66 Ministries, which is dedicated to helping people read and understand the Bible chronologically. She holds a Master's degree in Biblical Studies and plans to pursue a doctorate. When not writing, she's most likely indulging in old school music and sitcoms or watching superhero and time travel movies.

Connect with her at cynthia@wordtruthlifebible.com or https://www.amazon.com/author/caustintucker.